CLASSIC SERMONS ON THE HOLY SPIRIT

KREGEL CLASSIC SERMONS Series

- Classic Sermons on the Apostle Paul
- Classic Sermons on the Apostle Peter
- Classic Sermons on the Attributes of God
- Classic Sermons on the Birth of Christ
- Classic Sermons on Christian Service
- Classic Sermons on the Cross of Christ
- Classic Sermons on Faith and Doubt
- Classic Sermons on Family and Home
- Classic Sermons on Heaven and Hell
- Classic Sermons on the Holy Spirit
- Classic Sermons on Hope
- Classic Sermons on Judas Iscariot
- Classic Sermons on the Miracles of Jesus
- Classic Sermons on the Names of God
- Classic Sermons on Overcoming Fear
- Classic Sermons on Praise
- Classic Sermons on Prayer
- Classic Sermons on the Prodigal Son
- Classic Sermons on the Resurrection of Christ
- Classic Sermons on Revival and Spiritual Renewal
- Classic Sermons on the Second Coming and Other Prophetic Themes
- Classic Sermons on the Sovereignty of God
- Classic Sermons on Spiritual Warfare
- Classic Sermons on Suffering
- Classic Sermons on Worship

KREGEL CLASSIC SERMONS SERIES

CLASSIC SERMONS ON THE HOLY SPIRIT

Compiled by
Warren W. Wiersbe

Grand Rapids, MI 49501

Classic Sermons on the Holy Spirit
Compiled by Warren W. Wiersbe

Copyright © 1996 by Kregel Publications. All rights reserved. No part of this book may be reproduced, stored in a retrieval system, or transmitted in any form or by any means—electronic, mechanical, photocopy, recording, or otherwise—without written permission of the publisher, except for brief quotations in printed reviews.

Published by Kregel Publications, a division of Kregel, Inc., P.O. Box 2607, Grand Rapids, MI 49501. Kregel Publications provides trusted, biblical publications for Christian growth and service. Your comments and suggestions are valued.

Cover photo: © 1996, COMSTOCK INC.
Cover and book design: Alan G. Hartman

Library of Congress Cataloging-in-Publication Data

Classic sermons on the Holy Spirit / [compiled by] Warren W. Wiersbe.
    p.   cm.— (Kregel classic sermons series)
  Includes index.
  1. Holy Spirit—Sermons. 2. Holy Spirit—Biblical teaching—Sermons. 3. Baptists—Sermons
4. Sermons, American. 5. Sermons, English.
I. Title. II. Series
BT122.W54   1996   231'.3—dc20   96-10342
                                                                                 CIP

ISBN   0-8254-4076-9

Printed in the United States of America
1 2 3 4 5 / 00 99 98 97 96

CONTENTS

List of Scripture Texts 6
Preface 7
1. The Holy Spirit's Intercession 9
   Charles Haddon Spurgeon
2. He "Pours Forth" the Spirit 29
   William E. Sangster
3. The Spirit's Office toward Disciples 39
   Charles Haddon Spurgeon
4. Is the Spirit of the Lord Straitened? 53
   Alexander Maclaren
5. Belated Saints 63
   Clovis Gillham Chappell
6. The Holy Spirit through Christ, in the
   Church, for the World 73
   G. Campbell Morgan
7. The Spirit's Work in Believers 87
   Charles Simeon
8. On Grieving the Holy Spirit 103
   John Wesley
9. What God the Spirit Can Do for Us 113
   Howard Frederick Sugden
10. The Work of the Spirit 127
    Robert Murray McCheyne
11. The Holy Spirit Our Teacher 137
    Joseph Barber Lightfoot
12. The Wind of the Spirit 147
    James S. Stewart

LIST OF SCRIPTURE TEXTS

Genesis 1:2, McCheyne 127
Micah 2:7, Maclaren 53
John 3:8, Stewart 147
John 16:13–14, Lightfoot 137
John 16:14, Spurgeon 39
Acts 2:33, Morgan 73
Acts 2:33, Sangster 29
Acts 18:25, Chappell 63
Romans 8:9, Simeon 87
Romans 8:26–27, Spurgeon 9
Ephesians 4:30, Wesley 103

PREFACE

THE *KREGEL CLASSIC SERMONS SERIES* is an attempt to assemble and publish meaningful sermons from master preachers about significant themes.

These are *sermons*, not essays or chapters taken from books about themes. Not all of these sermons could be called great, but all of them are *meaningful*. They apply the truths of the Bible to the needs of the human heart, which is something that all effective preaching must do.

While some are better known than others, all of the preachers whose sermons I have selected had important ministries and were highly respected in their day. The fact that a sermon is included in this volume does not mean that either the compiler or the publisher agrees with or endorses everything that the man did, preached, or wrote. The sermon is here because it has a valued contribution to make.

These are sermons about *significant* themes. The pulpit is no place to play with trivia. The preacher has thirty minutes in which to help mend broken hearts, change defeated lives, and save lost souls; he can never accomplish this demanding ministry by distributing homiletical tidbits. In these difficult days we do not need clever pulpiteers who discuss the times; we need dedicated ambassadors who will preach the eternities.

The reading of these sermons can enrich your spiritual life. The studying of them can enrich your skills as an interpreter and expounder of God's truth. However God uses these sermons in your life and ministry, my prayer is that His church around the world will be encouraged and strengthened by them.

WARREN W. WIERSBE

The Holy Spirit's Intercession

Charles Haddon Spurgeon (1834–1892) is undoubtedly the most famous minister of the nineteenth century. Converted in 1850, he united with the Baptists and soon began to preach in various places. He became pastor of the Baptist church in Waterbeach, England, in 1851, and three years later he was called to the decaying Park Street Church, London. Within a short time the work began to prosper, a new church was built and dedicated in 1861, and Spurgeon became London's most popular preacher. In 1855, he began to publish his sermons weekly; today they make up the fifty-seven volumes of *The Metropolitan Tabernacle Pulpit*. He founded a pastor's college and several orphanages.

This sermon is taken from *The Metropolitan Tabernacle Pulpit*, volume 26.

Charles Haddon Spurgeon

1

THE HOLY SPIRIT'S INTERCESSION

> Likewise the Spirit also helpeth our infirmities: for we know not what we should pray for as we ought: but the Spirit itself maketh intercession for us with groanings which cannot be uttered. And he that searcheth the hearts knoweth what is the mind of the Spirit, because he maketh intercession for the saints according to the will of God (Romans 8:26–27).

THE APOSTLE PAUL WAS writing to a tried and afflicted people, and one of his objects was to remind them of the rivers of that which were flowing near at hand. He first of all stirred up their pure minds by way of remembrance as to their sonship—for he says, "as many as are led by the Spirit of God, they are the sons of God" (Rom. 8:14). They were, therefore, encouraged to take part and lot with Christ, the elder brother, with whom they had become joint heirs. They were exhorted to suffer with Him that they might afterward be glorified with Him. All that they endured came from a Father's hand and this should comfort them. A thousand sources of joy are opened in that one blessing of adoption. Blessed be the God and Father of our Lord Jesus Christ by whom we have been begotten into the family of grace.

When Paul had alluded to that consoling subject he turned to the next ground of comfort, namely, that we are to be sustained under present trial by hope. There is an amazing glory in reserve for us, and though as yet we cannot enter upon it but in harmony with the whole creation must continue to groan and travail, yet the hope itself should minister strength to us and enable us patiently to bear "this light affliction, which is but for a moment" (2 Cor. 4:17). This also is a truth full of sacred refreshment: hope sees a crown in reserve, mansions in readiness, and Jesus Himself preparing a place for us, and by the rapturous sight hope sustains the soul under the sorrows of the hour. Hope is the grand anchor by which means we ride out the present storm.

The apostle then turns to a third source of comfort, namely, the abiding of the Holy Spirit in and with the Lord's people. Paul uses the word *likewise* to intimate that in the same manner as hope sustains the soul, so does the Holy Spirit strengthen us under trial. Hope operates spiritually upon our spiritual faculties, and so does the Holy Spirit, in some mysterious way, divinely operate upon the newborn faculties of the believer, so that he is sustained under his infirmities. In His light shall we see light: I pray, therefore, that we may be helped of the Spirit while we consider His mysterious operations, that we may not fall into error or miss precious truth through blindness of heart.

The text speaks of "our infirmities," or, as many translators put it, in the singular—of "our infirmity." By this is intended our affliction and the weakness that trouble discovers in us. The Holy Spirit helps us to bear the infirmity of our bodies and of our minds; He helps us to bear our cross, whether it be physical pain or mental depression or spiritual conflict or slander or poverty or persecution. He helps our infirmity, and with a helper so divinely strong we need not fear for the result. God's grace will be sufficient for us; His strength will be made perfect in weakness.

I think, dear friends, you will all admit that if a man can pray, his trouble is at once lightened. When we feel that we have power with God and can obtain anything we ask for at His hands, then our difficulties cease to oppress us. We take our burden to our heavenly Father and tell it out in the accents of childlike confidence, and we come away quite content to bear whatever His holy will may lay upon us. Prayer is a great outlet for grief; it draws up the sluices and abates the swelling flood, which else might be too strong for us. We bathe the wound in the lotion of prayer and the pain is lulled, the fever is removed. But the worst of it is that in certain conditions of heart we cannot pray. We may be brought into such perturbation of mind and perplexity of heart that we do not know how to pray. We see the mercy seat and perceive that God will hear us; we have no doubt about that, for we know that we are His own favored children, and yet we hardly know what to desire. We fall into such heaviness of spirit and entanglement of thought that the one remedy of prayer, which we have always found to be unfailing, appears to be taken from us. Here, then, in the nick of time, as a very present help in time of trouble, comes in the Holy Spirit. He draws near to teach us how to pray, and in this way He helps our infirmity, relieves our suffering, and enables us to bear the heavy burden without fainting under the load.

At this time our subjects for consideration shall be, firstly, *the help that the Holy Spirit gives*; secondly, *the prayers that He inspires*; and thirdly, *the success that such prayers are certain to obtain.*

The Help That the Holy Spirit Gives

The help that the Holy Spirit renders to us *meets the weakness that we deplore*. As I have already said, if in time of trouble a man can pray, his burden loses its weight. If the believer can take anything and everything to God, then he learns to glory in infirmity and to rejoice in tribulation, but sometimes we are in such confusion of mind that we know not what we should pray for as we ought. In a measure, through our ignorance, we never know what we should pray for until we are taught of the Spirit of God. But there are times when this beclouding of the soul is dense indeed, and we do not even know what would help us out of our trouble if we could obtain it. We see the disease, but the name of the medicine is not known to us. We look over the many things that we might ask for of the Lord; we feel that each of them would be helpful, but that none of them would precisely meet our case. For spiritual blessings which we know to be according to the divine will we could ask with confidence, but perhaps these would not meet our peculiar circumstances. There are other things for which we are allowed to ask, but we scarcely know whether, if we had them, they would really serve our turn. We also feel a diffidence as to praying for them. In praying for temporal things we plead with measured voices, ever referring our petitions for revision to the will of the Lord. Moses prayed that he might enter Canaan, but God denied him; the man that was healed asked our Lord that he might be with Him, but he received for an answer, Go home to thy friends. We pray evermore on such matters with this reserve, "Nevertheless, not as I will, but as thou wilt" (Matt. 26:39). At times this very spirit of resignation appears to increase our mental difficulty for we do not wish to ask for anything that would be contrary to the mind of God, and yet we must ask for something. We are reduced to such straits that we must pray, but what shall be the particular subject of prayer we cannot for awhile make out. Even when ignorance and perplexity are removed, we know not what we should pray for as we ought.

When we know the matter of prayer, we yet fail to pray in a right manner. We ask, but we are afraid that we shall not have because we do not exercise the thought or the faith that we judge to be essential to prayer. We cannot at times command even the earnestness that is the life of supplication. A torpor steals over us, the heart is chilled, the hand is numbed, and we cannot wrestle with the angel. We know what to pray for as to objects, but we do not know what to pray for as we ought. It is the manner of the prayer that perplexes us, even when the matter is decided upon. How can I pray? My mind wanders; I chatter like a crane; I roar like a beast in pain; I moan in the brokenness of my heart, but oh, my God, I know not what it is my inmost spirit needs. Or if I know it, I know not how to frame my petition aright before You. I know not how to open my lips in Your majestic presence. I am so troubled that I cannot speak. My spiritual distress robs me of the power to pour out my heart before my God.

Now, beloved, it is in such a plight as this that the Holy Spirit aids us with His divine help; hence, He is a very present help in time of trouble (see Ps. 46:1).

Coming to our aid in our bewilderment *He instructs us*. This is one of His frequent operations upon the mind of the believer: "he shall teach you all things" (John 14:26). He instructs us as to our need and as to the promises of God that refer to that need. He shows us where our deficiencies are, what our sins are, and what our necessities are. He sheds a light upon our condition and makes us feel deeply our helplessness, sinfulness, and dire poverty. Then He casts the same light upon the promises of the Word and lays home to the heart that very text that was intended to meet the occasion—the precise promise that was framed with foresight of our present distress. In that light He makes the promise shine in all its truthfulness, certainty, sweetness, and suitability, so that we, poor trembling sons of men, dare take that word into our mouths which first came out of God's mouth, and then come with it as an argument and plead it before the throne of the heavenly grace. Our prevalence in prayer lies in the plea, "Lord, do as Thou hast said." How greatly we ought to value the Holy Spirit because when we are in the dark He gives us light. When our perplexed spirits are so befogged and beclouded that we cannot see our own need and cannot find out the appropriate promise in the Scriptures, the Spirit of God comes in and teaches us all things, and brings all things to our remembrance, whatsoever our Lord has told us. He guides us in prayer, and thus He helps our infirmity.

But the blessed Spirit does more than this. He often *directs the mind to the special subject of prayer*. He dwells within us as a counselor and points out to us what it is we should seek at the hands of God. We do not know why it is so, but we sometimes find our minds carried as by a strong undercurrent into a particular line of prayer for some one definite object. It is not merely that our judgment leads us in that direction, though usually the Spirit of God acts upon us by enlightening our judgment, but we often feel an unaccountable and irresistible desire rising again and again within our hearts. This so presses upon us that we not only utter the desire before God at our ordinary times for prayer, but we feel it crying in our hearts all the day long, almost to the supplanting of all other considerations. At such times we should thank God for direction and give our desire a clear road. The Holy Spirit is granting us inward direction as to how we should order our petitions before the throne of grace, and we may now reckon upon good success in our pleadings. Such guidance will the Spirit give to each of you if you will ask Him to illuminate you. He will guide you both negatively and positively. Negatively, He will forbid you to pray for such and such a thing, even as Paul essayed to go into Bithynia but the Spirit suffered him not. On the other hand, He will cause you to hear a cry within your soul that shall guide your petitions, even as he made Paul hear the cry from Macedonia saying, "Come over and help us." The Spirit teaches wisely as no other teacher can do. Those who obey His promptings shall not walk in darkness. He leads the spiritual eye to take good and steady aim at the very center of the target, and thus we hit the mark in our pleadings.

Nor is this all, for the Spirit of God is not sent merely to guide and help our devotion, but He Himself "maketh intercession for us" according to the will of God. By this expression it cannot be meant that the Holy Spirit ever groans or personally prays, but that He *excites intense desire and creates unutterable groanings in us*, and these are ascribed to Him. Even as Solomon built the temple because he superintended and ordained all, and yet I know not that he ever fashioned a timber or prepared a stone, so does the Holy Spirit pray and plead within us by leading us to pray and plead. This He does by arousing our desires. The Holy Spirit has a wonderful power over renewed hearts, as much power as the skillful minstrel has over the strings among which he lays his accustomed hand. The influences of the Holy Spirit at times pass through the soul like winds through an eolian harp, creating and inspiring sweet notes of gratitude and tones of desire to which we should have been strangers if it had not been for His divine visitation. He knows how to create in our spirits hunger and thirst for good things. He can arouse us from our spiritual lethargy; He can warm us out of our lukewarmness; He can enable us when we are on our knees to rise above the ordinary routine of prayer into that victorious importunity against which nothing can stand. He can lay certain desires so pressingly upon our hearts that we can never rest until they are fulfilled. He can make the zeal for God's house to eat us up and the passion for God's glory to be like a fire within our bones. This is one part of that process by which in inspiring our prayers He helps our infirmity. True Advocate is He, and Comforter most effectual. Blessed be His name.

The Holy Spirit also divinely operates in the *strengthening of the faith of believers*. That faith is at first of His creating, and afterward it is of His sustaining and increasing. Oh, brothers and sisters, have you not often felt your faith rise in proportion to your trials? Have you not, like Noah's ark, mounted toward heaven as the flood deepened around you? You have felt as sure about the promise as you felt about the trial. The affliction was, as it were, in your very bones, but the promise was also in your very heart. You could not doubt the affliction, for you smarted under it. But you might almost as soon have doubted that you were afflicted as have doubted the divine help, for your confidence was firm and unmoved. The greatest faith is only what God has a right to expect from us; yet do we never exhibit it except as the Holy Spirit strengthens our confidence and opens up before us the covenant with all its seals and securities. He it is that leads our souls to cry, "Although my house be not so with God; yet he hath made with me an everlasting covenant, ordered in all things, and sure" (2 Sam. 23:5). Blessed be the Divine Spirit then that, since faith is essential to prevailing prayer, He helps us in supplication by increasing our faith. Without faith prayer cannot speed, for he that wavers is like a wave of the sea driven with the wind and tossed, and such a one may not expect anything of the Lord. Happy are we when the Holy Spirit removes our wavering and enables us, like Abraham, to believe without staggering, knowing full well that He who has promised is able also to perform.

By three figures I will endeavor to describe the work of the Spirit of God in this matter—though they all fall short, and indeed all that I can say must fall infinitely short of the glory of His work. The actual mode of His working upon the mind we may not attempt to explain; it remains a mystery and it would be an unholy intrusion to attempt to remove the veil. There is no difficulty in our believing that as one human mind operates upon another mind, so does the Holy Spirit influence our spirits. We are forced to use words if we would influence our fellowmen, but the Spirit of God can operate upon the human mind more directly and communicate with it in silence. Into that matter, however, we will not dive lest we intrude where our knowledge would be drowned by our presumption.

My illustrations do not touch the mystery, but set forth the grace. The Holy Spirit acts to His people somewhat *as a prompter to a reciter*. A man has to deliver a piece that he has learned, but his memory is treacherous. Therefore, somewhere out of sight there is a prompter, so that when the speaker is at a loss and might use a wrong word, a whisper is heard that suggests the right one. When the speaker has almost lost the thread of his discourse, he turns his ear and the prompter gives him the catchword that aids his memory. If I may be allowed the simile, I would say that this represents in part the work of the Spirit of God in us— suggesting to us the right desire and bringing all things to our remembrance whatsoever Christ has told us. In prayer we should often come to a dead stand, but He incites, suggests, and inspires, and so we go onward. In prayer we might grow weary, but the Comforter encourages and refreshes us with cheering thoughts.

When, indeed, we are in our bewilderment almost driven to give up prayer, the whisper of His love drops a live coal from off the altar into our souls, and our hearts glow with greater ardor than before. Regard the Holy Spirit as your prompter, and let your ear be opened to His voice.

But He is much more than this. Let me attempt a second simile: He is *as an advocate to one in peril at law*. Suppose that a poor man had a great lawsuit, touching his whole estate, and he was forced personally to go into court and plead his own cause and speak up for his rights. If he were an uneducated man, he would be in a poor plight. An adversary in the court might plead against him and overthrow him, for he could not answer him. This poor man knows very little about the law and is quite unable to meet his cunning opponent. Suppose one who was perfect in the law should take up his cause warmly, and come and live with him, and use all his knowledge so as to prepare his case for him, draw up his petitions for him, and fill his mouth with arguments—would not that be a grand relief? This counselor would suggest the line of pleading, arrange the arguments, and put them into right courtly language. When the poor man was baffled by a question asked in court, he would run home and ask his adviser. This adviser would then tell him exactly how to meet the objector. Suppose, too, that when he had to plead with the judge himself, this advocate at home should teach him how to behave and what to urge and encourage him to hope that he would prevail—would not this be a great boon? Who would be the pleader in such a case? The poor client would plead, but still, when he won the suit, he would trace it all to the advocate who lived at home and gave him counsel. Indeed, it would be the advocate pleading for him, even while he pleaded himself. This is an instructive emblem of a great fact. Within this narrow house of my body, this tenement of clay, if I be a true believer, there dwells the Holy Spirit. When I desire to pray I may ask Him what I should pray for as I ought, and He will help me. He will write the prayers that I ought to offer upon the tablets of my heart. I shall see them there, and so I shall be taught how to plead. It will be the Spirit's own self pleading in me and by me and through me before the throne of grace. What a happy man in his lawsuit would such a poor man be, and how happy are you and I that we have the Holy Spirit to be our Counselor!

Yet one more illustration: it is that *of a father aiding his boy*. Suppose it to be a time of war centuries back. Old English warfare was then conducted by bowmen to a great extent. Here is a youth who is to be initiated in the art of archery, and therefore he carries a bow. It is a strong bow and therefore very hard to draw; indeed, it requires more strength than the urchin can summon to bend it. See how his father teaches him. "Put your right hand here, my boy, and place your left hand so. Now pull." As the youth pulls, his father's hands are on his hands, and the bow is drawn. The lad draws the bow, yes, but it is quite as much his father, too. We cannot draw the bow of prayer alone. Sometimes a bow of steel is not broken by our hands, for we cannot even bend it; then the Holy Spirit puts His mighty hand over ours and covers our weakness so that we draw. Lo, what splendid drawing of the bow it is then! The bow bends so easily we wonder how it is. Away flies the arrow, and it pierces the very center of the target, for He who gives the strength directs the aim. We rejoice to think that we have won the day, but it was His secret might that made us strong and to Him be the glory of it.

Thus have I tried to set forth the cheering fact that the Spirit helps the people of God.

The Prayer That the Holy Spirit Inspires

The text says, "The Spirit itself maketh intercession for us with groanings which cannot be uttered." It is not the Spirit that groans, but we that groan. As I have shown you, the Spirit excites the emotion that causes us to groan.

It is clear, then, the prayers that are indited in us

by the Spirit of God are *those that arise from the inmost soul*. A man's heart is moved when he groans. A groan is a matter about which there is no hypocrisy. A groan comes not from the lips, but from the heart. A groan, then, is a part of prayer that we owe to the Holy Spirit, and the same is true of all the prayer that wells up from the deep fountains of the inner life. The prophet cried, "My bowels, my bowels! I am pained at my very heart; my heart maketh a noise in me." This deep groundswell of desire, this tidal motion of the lifefloods is caused by the Holy Spirit. His work is never superficial, but always deep and inward.

Such prayers will rise within us when the mind is far too troubled to let us speak. We know not what we should pray for as we ought, and then it is that we groan or utter some other inarticulate sound. Hezekiah said, "like a crane or a swallow did I chatter" (Isa. 38:14). The psalmist said, "I am so troubled that I cannot speak" (Ps. 77:4). In another place he said, "I am feeble and sore broken: I have roared by reason of the disquietness of my heart" (Ps. 38:8–9). But he added, "Lord, all my desire is before thee; and my groaning is not hid from thee." The sighing of the prisoner surely comes up into the ears of the Lord. There is real prayer in these groanings that cannot be uttered. It is the power of the Holy Spirit in us that creates all real prayer, even that which takes the form of a groan because the mind is incapable, by reason of its bewilderment and grief, of clothing its emotion in words. I pray you never think lightly of the supplications of your anguish. Rather, judge that such prayers are like Jabez, of whom it is written, that he "was more honorable than his brethren, . . . because [his mother] bare him with sorrow" (1 Chron. 4:9). That which is thrown up from the depth of the soul, when it is stirred with a terrible tempest, is more precious than pearl or coral, for it is the intercession of the Holy Spirit.

These prayers are sometimes groanings that cannot be uttered because *they concern such great things that they cannot be spoken.* I want, my Lord! I want, I want;

I cannot tell You what I want, but I seem to want all things. If it were some little thing, my narrow capacity could comprehend and describe it, but I need all covenant blessings. You know what I have need of before I ask You. Though I cannot go into each item of my need, I know it to be very great and such as I myself can never estimate. I groan, for I can do no more. Prayers that are the offspring of great desires, sublime aspirations, and elevated designs are surely the work of the Holy Spirit, and their power within a man is frequently so great that he cannot find expression for them. Words fail, and even the sighs that try to embody them cannot be uttered.

But it may be, beloved, that we groan because we are conscious of the littleness of our desire and the narrowness of our faith. The trial, too, may seem too mean to pray about. I have known what it is to feel as if I could not pray about a certain matter, and yet I have been obliged to groan about it. A thorn in the flesh may be as painful a thing as a sword in the bones, and yet we may go and beseech the Lord thrice about it, and getting no answer we may feel that we know not what to pray for as we ought; yet it makes us groan. Yes, and with that natural groan there may go up an unutterable groaning of the Holy Spirit. Beloved, what a different view of prayer God has from that which men think to be the correct one. You may have seen very beautiful prayers in print, and you may have heard very charming compositions from the pulpit, but I trust you have not fallen in love with them. Judge these things rightly. I pray you never think well of fine prayers, for before the thrice holy God it ill becomes a sinful suppliant to play the orator.

We heard of a certain clergyman who was said to have given forth "the finest prayer ever offered to a Boston audience." Just so! The Boston audience received the prayer, and there it ended. We want the mind of the Spirit in prayer and not the mind of the flesh. The tail feathers of pride should be pulled out of our prayers, for they need only the wing feathers of faith; the peacock feathers of poetical expression are out of place before the throne of God. "Dear me, what remarkably beautiful language he used in prayer!" "What an intellectual treat his prayer was!" Yes, yes; but God looks at the heart. To Him fine language is as sounding brass or a tinkling cymbal, but a groan has music in it. *We* do not like groans. Our ears are much too delicate to tolerate such dreary sounds, but not so the great Father of spirits. A Methodist brother cries, "Amen," and you say, "I cannot bear such Methodistic noise"; no, but if it comes from the man's heart God can bear it. When you get upstairs into your chamber this evening to pray and find you cannot pray, but have to moan out, "Lord, I am too full of anguish and too perplexed to pray, hear the voice of my roaring," though you reach to nothing else you will be really praying. When, like David, we can say, "I opened my mouth, and panted" (Ps. 119:131), we are by no means in an ill state of mind. All fine language in prayer and especially all intoning or performing of prayers must be abhorrent to God. It is little short of profanity to offer solemn supplication to God after the manner called "intoning." The sighing of a true heart is infinitely more acceptable, for it is the work of the Spirit of God.

We may say of the prayers that the Holy Spirit works in us that they are *prayers of knowledge*. Notice, our difficulty is that we know not what we should pray for. But the Holy Spirit does know, and therefore He helps us by enabling us to pray intelligently, knowing what we are asking for, so far as this knowledge is needful to valid prayer. The text speaks of the "mind of the Spirit." What a mind that must be—the mind of that Spirit who arranged all the order that now pervades this earth! There was once chaos and confusion, but the Holy Spirit brooded over all, and His mind is the originator of that beautiful arrangement which we so admire in the visible creation. What a mind His must be! The Holy Spirit's mind is seen in our intercessions when under His sacred influence we order our case before the Lord and plead with holy wisdom for things convenient and necessary. What wise and admirable desires must those be that the Spirit of Wisdom Himself works in us!

Moreover, the Holy Spirit's intercession creates *prayers offered in a proper manner*. I showed you that the difficulty is that we know not what we should pray for as we ought, and the Spirit meets that difficulty by making intercession for us in a right manner. The Holy Spirit works in us humility, earnestness, intensity, importunity, faith, resignation, and all else that is acceptable to God in our supplications. We know not how to mingle these sacred spices in the incense of prayer. We, if left to ourselves, at our very best get too much of one ingredient or another and spoil the sacred compound, but the Holy Spirit's intercessions have in them such a blessed blending of all that is good that they come up as a sweet perfume before the Lord. Spirit-taught prayers are offered as they ought to be. They are His own intercession in some respects, for we read that the Holy Spirit not only helps us to intercede but "maketh intercession." It is twice over declared in our text that He makes intercession for us, and the meaning of this I tried to show when I described a father as putting his hands upon his child's hands. This is something more than helping us to pray, something more than encouraging us or directing us—but I venture no further, except to say that He puts such force of His own mind into our poor weak thoughts and desires and hopes that He Himself makes intercession for us, working in us to will and to pray according to His good pleasure.

I want you to notice, however, that *these intercessions of the Holy Spirit are only in the saints*. "He maketh intercession for us," and "He maketh intercession for the saints." Does He do nothing for sinners, then? Yes, He quickens sinners into spiritual life, and He strives with them to overcome their sinfulness and turn them into the right way. But in the saints He works with us and enables us to pray after His mind and according to the will of God. His intercession is not in or for the unregenerate. Oh, unbelievers, you must first be made saints or you cannot feel the Spirit's intercession within you. What need we have to go to Christ for the blessing of the Holy Spirit that is peculiar to the children of God and can only be ours by faith in Christ Jesus! "As many as received him, to them gave he power to become the sons of God" John 1:12); and to the sons of God alone comes the Spirit of adoption and all His helping grace. Unless we are the sons of God, the Holy Spirit's indwelling shall not be ours. We are shut out from the intercession of the Holy Spirit, yes, and from the intercession of Jesus too, for He has said, "I pray not for the world, but for them which thou hast given me" (John 17:9).

Thus I have tried to show you the kind of prayer which the Spirit inspires.

The Sure Success of All Such Prayers

All the prayers that the Spirit of God inspires in us must succeed, because, first, *there is a meaning in them that God reads and approves*. When the Spirit of God writes a prayer upon a man's heart, the man himself may be in such a state of mind that he does not altogether know what it is. His interpretation of it is a groan and that is all. Perhaps he does not even get so far as that in expressing the mind of the Spirit. He feels groanings that he cannot utter; he cannot find a door of utterance for his inward grief. Yet our heavenly Father, who looks immediately upon the heart, reads what the Spirit of God has indited there and does not need even our groans to explain the meaning. He reads the heart itself: he knoweth, says the text, "what is the mind of the Spirit." The Spirit is one with the Father, and the Father knows what the Spirit means. The desires that the Spirit prompts may be too spiritual for such babes in grace as we are actually to describe or to express, and yet they are within us. We feel desires for things that we should never have thought of if He had not made us long for them—aspirations for blessings that as to the understanding of them are still above us, yet the Spirit writes the desire on the renewed mind, and the Father sees it.

Now that which God reads in the heart and approves of—for the word to "know" in this case includes approval as well as the mere act of omniscience—in the heart must succeed. Did not Jesus say, "Your Father knoweth what things you have need of before you ask him" (Matt. 6:8)? Did He not tell us this as an encouragement to believe that we shall receive all needful blessings? So it is with those prayers that are all broken up, wet with tears, and discordant with sighs and inarticulate expressions and heavings of the bosom and sobbings of the heart and anguish and bitterness of spirit. Our gracious Lord reads them as a man reads a book, and they are written in a character that He fully understands. To give a simple figure: if I were to come into your house I might find there a little child that cannot yet speak plainly. It cries for something, and it makes very odd and objectionable noises, combined with signs and movements that are almost meaningless to a stranger. But his mother understands him and attends to his little pleadings. A mother can translate babytalk; she comprehends incomprehensible noises. Even so does our Father in heaven know all about our poor baby talk, for our prayer is not much better. He knows and comprehends the cryings and moanings and sighings and chatterings of His bewildered children. Yes, a tender mother knows her child's needs before the child knows what it wants. Perhaps the little one stutters, stammers, and cannot get its words out, but the mother sees what he would say and takes the meaning. Even so, we know concerning our great Father—

> He knows the thoughts we mean to speak,
> Ere from our opening lips they break.

Do you therefore rejoice in this, that because the prayers of the Spirit are known and understood of God, therefore they will be sure to speed.

The next argument for making us sure that they will speed is this—that *they are "the mind of the Spirit."*

God the ever blessed is one, and there can be no division between the Father, the Son, and the Holy Spirit. These divine persons always work together, and there is a common desire for the glory of each blessed Person of the Divine Unity. Therefore it cannot be conceived without profanity that anything could be the mind of the Holy Spirit and not be the mind of the Father and the mind of the Son. The mind of God is one and harmonious. If, therefore, the Holy Spirit dwells in you and moves you to any desire, then His mind is in your prayer, and it is not possible that the eternal Father should reject your petitions. That prayer that came from heaven will certainly go back to heaven. If the Holy Spirit prompts it, the Father must and will accept it, for it is not possible that He should put a slight upon the ever blessed and adorable Spirit.

But one more word and that closes the argument, namely, that *the work of the Spirit in the heart is not only the mind of the Spirit which God knows, but it is also according to the will or mind of God*, for He never makes intercession in us other than is consistent with the divine will. Now, the divine will or mind may be viewed two ways. First, there is the will declared in the proclamations of holiness by the Ten Commandments. The Spirit of God never prompts us to ask for anything that is unholy or inconsistent with the precepts of the Lord. Then, secondly, there is the secret mind of God, the will of His eternal predestination and decree, of which we know nothing. But we do know this, that the Spirit of God never prompts us to ask anything that is contrary to the eternal purpose of God. Reflect for a moment: the Holy Spirit knows all the purposes of God. When they are about to be fulfilled, He moves the children of God to pray about them, and so their prayers keep touch and tally with the divine decrees. Oh, would you not pray confidently if you knew that your prayer corresponded with the sealed book of destiny? We may safely entreat the Lord to do what He has Himself ordained to do. A carnal man draws the inference that if God has ordained an event we need not pray about it. But faith obediently draws the inference that the God who secretly ordained to give the blessing has openly commanded that we should pray for it, and therefore faith obediently prays. Coming events cast their shadows before them, and when God is about to bless His people His coming favor casts the shadow of prayer over the church. When He is about to favor an individual He casts the shadow of hopeful expectation over his soul. Our prayers—let men laugh at them as they will and say there is no power in them—are the indicators of the movement of the wheels of Providence. Believing supplications are forecasts of the future. He who prays in faith is like the seer of old, he sees that which is yet to be. His holy expectancy, like a telescope, brings distant objects near to him and things not seen as yet are visible to him. He is bold to declare that he has the petition that he has asked of God, and he therefore begins to rejoice and to praise God even before the blessing has actually arrived. So it is: prayer prompted by the Holy Spirit is the footfall of the divine decree.

I conclude by saying, see, my dear hearers, the absolute necessity of the Holy Spirit. For if the saints know not what they should pray for as they ought; if consecrated men and women, with Christ suffering in them, still feel their need of the instruction of the Holy Spirit, how much more do you who are not saints and have never given yourselves up to God require divine teaching! Oh, that you would know and feel your dependence upon the Holy Spirit that He may prompt you this day to look to Jesus Christ for salvation. It is through the once crucified but now ascended Redeemer that this gift of the Spirit, this promise of the Father, is shed abroad upon men. May He who comes from Jesus lead you to Jesus.

And, then, O people of God, let this last thought abide with you—what condescension is this that this Divine Person should dwell in you forever and that He should be with you to help your prayers. Listen to me for a moment. If I read in the Scriptures that in the most heroic acts of faith God the Holy Spirit helps His people, I can understand it; if I read that in the sweetest music of their songs when they worship best and chant their loftiest strains before the most high God, the Spirit helps them, I can understand it; and even if I hear that in their wrestling prayers and prevalent intercessions God the Holy Spirit helps them, I can understand it. But I bow with reverent amazement, my heart sinking into the dust with adoration, when I reflect that God the Holy Spirit helps us when we cannot speak but can only groan. Yes, and when we cannot even utter our groanings, He does not only help us but He claims as His own particular creation the groanings that cannot be uttered. This is condescension indeed! In deigning to help us in the grief that cannot even vent itself in groaning, He proves Himself to be a true Comforter. O God, my God, You have not forsaken me. You are not far from me nor from the voice of my roaring. You did for awhile leave Your Firstborn when He was made a curse for us, so that He cried in agony, "Why hast thou forsaken me?" (Matt. 27:46). But You will not leave any of the many brethren for whom He died. Your Spirit shall be with them, and when they cannot so much as groan He will make intercession for them with groanings that cannot be uttered. God bless you, my beloved brethren, and may you feel the Spirit of the Lord thus working in you and with you. Amen and amen.

He "Pours Forth" the Spirit

William E. Sangster (1900–1960) was the "John Wesley of his generation" as he devoted his life to evangelism and the promotion of practical sanctification. He pastored in England and Wales, and his preaching ability attracted the attention of the Methodist leaders. He ministered during World War II at Westminster Central Hall, London, where he pastored the church, managed an air-raid shelter in the basement, and studied for his Ph.D. at the London University. He served as president of the Methodist Conference (1950) and director of the denomination's home missions and evangelism ministry. He published several books on preaching, sanctification, and evangelism, as well as volumes of sermons.

This message comes from *Westminster Sermons*, volume 2, published in 1961 by Epworth Press, London.

William E. Sangster

2

HE "POURS FORTH" THE SPIRIT

> Being therefore by the right hand of God exalted, and having received of the Father the promise of the Holy Ghost, he hath poured forth this . . . (Acts 2:33 RV).

WE HAVE COME TO the day of Pentecost and, therefore, to the birthday of the church, for the church was born when the Holy Spirit was given.

We are told in our text that when Jesus was exalted, He "poured forth" the Holy Spirit and it is of a special part of the work of the Holy Spirit that I want to speak now.

The Holy Spirit is referred to in the New Testament by various terms and, among others, by the term *paraclete*. The word *paraclete* comes from two simple Greek words: *para*, which (in this connection) means "alongside," and *kaleo*, which means "to call" or "to summon." The word is usually employed in the context of a court of law. So you get the picture: one "called alongside of," and the word is sometimes translated "comforter," and sometimes "counselor," but best of all it is translated "advocate."

In legal English the word means "barrister." They seldom use the word *barrister* in Scotland. For the same office they use the better term *advocate*, and it is with the Holy Spirit as an Advocate that I am concerned now.

The function of an advocate at any time is to plead. It is an office of distinction. If some woman you knew were going to marry a barrister (or advocate) you—because, like most other people, you may have a way of assessing people not at their real worth, but by the kind of work they do—would be disposed to think that she was marrying well.

There is, of course, a professional code operative with advocates. It has two chief principles. Just as there is a bond of absolute secrecy between a minister and the members of the flock when they come to speak of their spiritual needs or confess their sins, just as there is a bond of absolute secrecy between a doctor and the patient in all that concerns the patient's health, so the relationship between the advocate and the client is absolutely confidential too. Not even a court of law can compel the disclosure of any communication that takes place between them. The prisoner can speak his whole mind to his advocate, and the advocate will hold it in absolute confidence.

And the other great duty of an advocate is that he must do his best for his client at all costs. It may be that, in his private conversations with the man he is representing, admissions are made or hints are given that leave the advocate uncertain as to his client's integrity. Indeed, his piercing brain might even conclude that, on terms of strict justice, there isn't much to be said for the man. Nevertheless, his professional calling and his advocate's honor require that he does his best for him, his very best.

Carry that truth over to the high office of the Holy Spirit as Advocate, for in the New Testament that is one of His exalted names.

The Holy Spirit Pleads with Us

Notice, first, that He is an Advocate when He pleads *with* us.

> Christ is our Advocate on high;
> Thou art our Advocate within:
> O plead the truth, and make reply
> To every argument of sin.

The arguments of sin? What does that mean?

The psychologist (with a love of awkward phrases) calls it "the rationalization of desire." What does he mean by that? I can tell you.

Maybe next Sunday, when it is time for worship, you

will look out of the window and find that it is a beautiful day, and you begin to think like this:

"Of course, it is right to go to worship. I have a duty to my soul and to God. But, then, I have a duty to my body as well, and I have been cramped up in the office all week. What I really need is a change of air.

"Yes, and, moreover, there is old Bill down at the coast. Now, Bill must be very depressed having a holiday on his own with no one to cheer him up. Surely it is my duty as a friend to go down and see dear old Bill?

"And, of course, I need not neglect my soul entirely. I can read some nice, improving book in the train or take it with me in the car. That will probably do me more good than being in church. . . ."

You see how it runs? That is what the psychologist calls the rationalization of desire, and that is what the hymn writer had in mind when he spoke of the "argument of sin."

David knew it.

I think it would be difficult to get into little space all the evil that David crowded into the great sin of his life. He wanted the wife of one of his officers. He saw her and saw that she was beautiful. While his army was on active service fighting the king's battles, David seduced the woman. Then, fearing the consequences, he arranged the death of her husband and added murder to royal lust. The man after God's own heart wallowed in sin!

How did he ever get there?

This way. By the rationalization of desire. By the arguments of sin.

This is how it happened. A sinful thought crossed his mind, and this he could not help. But he dwelt on it when he should have blacked it out. He fed his imagination on it when he should have killed it with a prayer. He told himself that Uriah, the woman's husband, had died in the discharge of his duty. Gallant soldiers do fall, of course, on the field of battle! And then he married the woman and that, of course, as any lying adulterer knows, is supposed to rub the adultery out. He was a victim of the arguments of sin.

Look at me in the face and tell me: do you know anything about the arguments of sin?

Something tells me that you do.

Tell me this also: when, in the court of your soul, evil desire began to plead the arguments of sin, was there no other voice in that court pleading for *noble* things? Wasn't there a voice, low but clear and insistent, speaking to you of the best that you had ever been taught at home, in church, by your good mother; pleading, pleading like a skillful advocate in front of a judge, bringing up every good point from the past that will help his case? Do you remember that in your own soul? Who was it? I'll tell you who it was. It was the blessed Paraclete. It was the Holy Spirit. He was pleading the truth and making reply to every argument of sin.

Where would I have been, where would you have been, but for that blessed Paraclete? If, at our first foolish fingering of sin; if, as soon as we were seduced in our hearts by desire; if, when our vagrant wishes ran after that suggestive image; if He had left us without a word—where should we have been?

If you are strong in virtue, if there is at least a little bit of your soul defended against the assaults of passion, if there is something saved still from the inroads of worldliness, it is all the work of the blessed Paraclete.

And listen! *He is always there.* You may grieve Him and turn a deaf ear to Him, and by not heeding Him, the voice may grow faint, but I don't believe He has left (*entirely* left!) any one of you.

Did you see the report of that case in the courts the other day? A member of the bar had to plead "invisibility" at the Sheffield Quarter Sessions because he was not wearing his wig and gown. That is one of the rules of our courts. Officially he is not present. There was a prisoner in the dock, and he wanted the barrister to plead for him, but the judge said that he could not see the barrister because, according to our laws, the judge can only see an advocate when he is properly attired.

What a position for the poor prisoner—dumb in the

presence of undeniable guilt, no one to plead for him, no one to say: "My Lord, think on the extenuating circumstances"; no one to say: "He has a good record; he didn't mean to do it."

The Holy Spirit will never desert you. You can drive Him away, but He will go unwillingly. He wants to plead with you. He knows the worst about you and He longs to save.

I am bold to say that there is not one of you here present tonight (whether you have accepted the offer of God in Christ or not), who, by the mercy of God, doesn't know something in your conscience of the work of the Holy Spirit as Advocate. He has pleaded with you!

The Holy Spirit Pleads in Us

Not only does He plead with us, He pleads *in* us. I mean this. Put quite simply, prayer is the heart of our religion. That is the fact of it. People say to me sometimes: "I am no theologian or philosopher. Put it simply to me, preacher. What is the real heart of this Christian religion? How do you grow in what you call 'grace and power'?"

Prayer is the heart of it.

I know that many of our ideas are confused concerning prayer. I know that people pray for things that can only come by work, and sometimes work for things that can only come by prayer.

A woman once told me that she was leaving the church and never coming back again. When I asked her why, she said that her little girl had sat for a scholarship and, as her mother, she had prayed hard that her little girl would pass. She not only had not passed, but she was at the bottom of the list! So that proved there was nothing in prayer, and the mother was not coming to church any more.

The folly of it! It doesn't look as though I had taught her much about prayer. I take the blame upon myself.

I knew her little girl. She couldn't have won a scholarship for love or money. She hadn't got the brains for that.

She was a charming girl; she will be grown up now. She is probably the "queen" of some nice home and making her man happy. But a scholarship—not on your life.

Yet think of her mother losing faith in prayer because of that.

And there are other people who only pray when they are in extremity. They look upon prayer as a strong drug that you only turn to when you are in urgent danger, like the man not used to the ways of churches on whom a minister called because he had heard that the man was ill.

When the minister was ready to go he said a little tentatively to the sick man: "Shall I offer a word of prayer before I go?"

And the pale fellow in the bed turned paler still and said:

"O! no, thank you; I'm not as bad as that."

What would you think of a friend who only turned up when he wanted something? But that is how a good many of us treat God. We ignore Him until we want something desperately for ourselves and then we pray.

All this proves that people's thought about prayer is muddled. But listen! Even when our thought about prayer is clear, what awful sloth we have in it. God forgive us, though prayer is the heart of our religion, what poor craftsmen most of us are at praying.

Did you ever spend sixpence on a book of helps to prayer? Did you ever stay up late—no, not to finish your novel—but to pray? Did you ever rise early—no, not just to start on an excursion, but to pray?

Now, here is our dilemma as I see it—our Christian dilemma. Our growth in Christ depends upon prayer—and yet we cannot pray. Not really! The longing to pray is not in us. We have to push ourselves to our knees. What a plight! The very thing we most need, we have such little desire for.

How can we escape from this impasse?

Go to God! Tell God the dilemma that you are in. Tell Him frankly. Tell Him you know you will never grow in spiritual things without prayer. Tell Him honestly, as you must, that you have no real appetite for it.

And listen—I'll tell you what He will do. He will do for you what our monarch in England would do for any poor wretch who was in a similar plight—He Himself will provide you with a counsel. He will!

The law of Britain will not allow any man to stand accused in a court of law without a professional advocate to plead his case. If the accused is unable to provide the advocate himself, the Crown assumes the responsibility.

And the King of Heaven will do more than that for you. He will provide you, not a king's or queen's Counsel, but the King of Kings' Counsel—the Paraclete, the Advocate, the blessed Holy Spirit. He will plead in you. He will put in you a passion, a flame of prayer. "The Spirit also helpeth our infirmity, for we know not how to pray as we ought" (RV). With passing time He may even give you the gift of infused prayer. You will know that you are being prayed through.

I do not say that this will happen every day. There may still be times when you must prod yourself to prayer, but I do say that increasingly the desire to pray will possess you and that, as you pray, your sense of power in prayer will so increase that your busiest day will seem a day ill spent unless it has included some time given to prayer.

And that is the second great task of the Holy Spirit as Advocate: He pleads in us.

The Holy Spirit Pleads through Us

The Holy Spirit pleads *with* us and *in* us and *through* us. He pleads through us to the world of men.

It says in the New Testament that one of the functions of the Advocate is to convict the world of sin. What need there is of that!

It is one of the tragedies of the times that there is no acute sense of sin. People do the most awful things and think nothing of it. They are guilty of the most ghastly unfaithfulness to their marriage vows; they take things that do not belong to them. To lie and hate and smear people seems, in many quarters, no longer to be wrong. It is only wrong to be found out.

O! that the Holy Spirit would plead through us and convict the world of sin.

Think of the folly of war! Are we free of war even yet? Will it never come back again? Are you sure?

You are *not* sure! The world is not yet convicted of the sin and insanity of war.

Or think of the widespread sin of pride. How people boast of things that are really gifts of God! Think of the intellectual snobbery—as though they gave themselves their brains. Or they boast of their birth—as though they chose their parents. What forms of foolish pride we witness day after day! But can you convince them of it?

I do not know. The very effort to do it on our own seems to label us as prigs. I think only the Holy Spirit can do it. O! that He would plead through us and convict the world of sin.

Let us ask Him to do it. He will begin by first pointing out to us, with loving firmness, the sins that still survive in our own souls, and He will then plead through us—by our lives more than our words—to make sin self-conscious in those with whom we come in contact.

I am a preacher but in nothing do I fail more completely in my preaching than in convicting people of sin. I come here week by week and, like some poor, stammering advocate, plead the case for my Lord. Yet I do not know how to convict people of sin. My words are not enough. I need something more than a ready tongue—I need the power of the Holy Spirit.

Nor is this a need of preachers only; you need it too.

Maybe you are working with people and living with people deep in sin and unaware of it, oozing self-satisfaction, strutting about and saying "What's the matter with *me?*"

How will you convince them?

You can't! Not alone! You need the Holy Spirit to plead through you.

Savior, it is the Day of Pentecost. Pour forth the Divine Advocate into all our needy hearts that He may plead *with* us, and *in* us, and *through* us. For Thy name's sake. Amen.

The Spirit's Office toward Disciples

Charles Haddon Spurgeon (1834–1892) is undoubtedly the most famous minister of the nineteenth century. Converted in 1850, he united with the Baptists and soon began to preach in various places. He became pastor of the Baptist church in Waterbeach, England, in 1851, and three years later he was called to the decaying Park Street Church, London. Within a short time the work began to prosper, a new church was built and dedicated in 1861, and Spurgeon became London's most popular preacher. In 1855, he began to publish his sermons weekly; today they make up the fifty-seven volumes of *The Metropolitan Tabernacle Pulpit*. He founded a pastor's college and several orphanages.

This sermon is taken from *The Metropolitan Tabernacle Pulpit*, volume 53.

Charles Haddon Spurgeon

3
THE SPIRIT'S OFFICE TOWARD DISCIPLES

> He shall glorify me: for he shall receive of mine, and shall show it unto you (John 16:14).

MANY PERSONS ARE ANXIOUSLY asking the question, "Are we partakers of the Holy Spirit?" With enlarged anxiety they reason thus, "We have felt certain inward emotions; there has been in us, we trust, a change of life. Eager are our desires for God and His grace; do these come of the Spirit of God? When we find a suggestion that appears to be holy in our souls, does it come from Him? When we are at any time filled with earnestness and pray or our souls have peculiar delight in considering divine things, may we say with truth that we are under the operation of the Holy Spirit?" I do not intend to go thoroughly into the resolution of these scruples; that would be too wide a subject for a short evening's discourse. But there is one point that may often relieve your perplexities. It appears, from the text, that it is the work and office and custom of the Holy Spirit to glorify Christ. If, therefore, with much strength and fervor in your soul you glorify Him, you may trust that it comes from the Spirit of God. But if there be anything in you that is derogatory to the character or person or glory of the Lord Jesus, it may either come from Satan or from your own corrupt mind. But from the Spirit of God it never did come, and it would be blasphemy to impute it to Him. Whatever you feel that lifts Christ on high in your soul comes of the Spirit. But whatever there may be that exalts self, or anything else in the place of Christ, come whence it may, from the Holy Spirit it never did proceed.

Let us then just handle this point. The Holy Spirit

glorifies Christ in His people. How does He do it, and how far may I judge that He is at work in me?

The Holy Spirit Humbles Us

One way in which the Holy Spirit glorifies Christ is this—He gives us more and more debasing views of our own selves. There are two Gods, as it were—one the true, the other the false. Self first mounts the throne in our hearts; the higher the throne of self is exalted, the lower must Christ go. Much of self, little of the Savior. With exalted views of self, self-power, or self-righteousness, then there are sure to be low views of Christ, but when self goes down, then Christ at once rises. It may be said of self, as John the Baptist once said of Christ and himself, "He must increase, but I must decrease" (John 3:30). If you have had shallow views of your own natural depravity, then you have had very shallow thoughts of Christ. If you think sin to be delightful, if Gethsemane and Golgotha and Calvary seem to you to be names without weight or meaning, if you have never groaned under sin, I do not wonder that you think little of Christ's groans and griefs and bloody sweat. But when you come to know yourself as verily lost and undone, then you will prize your Deliverer. When the dread word *lost* has seemed to fall like a death knell upon your ear, then the tidings that the Son of Man came to seek and to save that which was lost will be sweet to you as the Christmas carol of the angels when they sang, "Glory to God in the highest, and on earth peace, good will toward men" (Luke 2:14). If you feel the disease, you will value the Physician; if you know your own emptiness, you will prize Christ's fullness. But if you reject the teaching of the Holy Spirit, which shows you your utter helplessness and worthlessness, in so doing you have rejected Christ and put far from you that Savior who alone came to save sinners. It is, then, a most precious thing when we begin to sink lower and lower in our own estimation. At the commencement of spiritual life, we believe that we are nothing; as we advance, we find that we are less than nothing. May the

Holy Spirit so work in you! Some of you are, perhaps, desponding and thinking that you are not children of God or else you would not be so cast down as you are. I pray you to understand this matter aright. Instead of having any reason for despondency, you will find a subject for joy, for sure I am that the Spirit is honoring Christ when He is lowering you in your own estimation.

The Holy Spirit Honors Christ

Still more to the point, when the Holy Spirit really works in the heart of man, He honors Christ in every respect.

He honors the person of Christ. Those who think but little of His deity are not taught of the Spirit of God. No man is taught by the Holy Spirit to regard the only-begotten Son of the Father as a secondary God, for the Holy Spirit teaches us upon this wise, "When he bringeth in the firstbegotten into the world, he saith, And let all the angels of God worship him" (Heb. 1:6). "In the beginning was the Word, and the Word was with God, and the Word was God" (John 1:1). The Spirit ever teaches concerning Christ that He is God over all, blessed forever. Some have had lowering views of His humanity. Every now and then we hear dark hints about the human nature of our Lord Jesus Christ, His peccability, and so on, but this never comes from the Spirit of God. Both the deity and the humanity of Christ receive honor in the Christian's soul when the Spirit comes there with light.

> Jesus is worthy to receive
> Honor, and power divine.

That very Man who did hang upon Calvary we now adore. He is exalted far above all principalities and powers. All teaching that honors Christ in His person is of the Spirit, but that which dishonors Him should be branded with its evil authorship.

The Spirit also glorifies Christ in His work. Have you ever seen the finished work of Christ? He came into the world to save men, and He did save them. He did not make a bridge over which they might possibly get across, but He carried them across the bridge. He did not so far accomplish the work of redemption that, by their own exertions, some persons might climb to heaven. He Himself entered into the heavenly places and took possession, representatively, of the throne of God for all His people who were in Him. The salvation of the elect, so far as Christ is concerned, is finished. He took upon His shoulders all their guilt; He was punished for that guilt; they were there and then justified. He rose again, having shaken off alike the punishment and the iniquities that incurred it; He entered into glory; they were there and then virtually made possessors of an inheritance that nothing will ever be able to take from them. Let the Christian feel that the teaching that lowers the work of Christ—makes it dependent upon the will of man as to its efficacy—puts the cross on the ground and says, "That blood is shed, but it may be shed in vain, shed in vain for you." Let us all feel that such teaching comes not from the Spirit of God. That teaching it is that, pointing to the cross, says, "He shall see of the travail of his soul, and shall be satisfied" (Isa. 53:11); that teaching that makes the atonement a true atonement which puts away the vindictive justice of God forever from every soul for whom that atonement was offered, exalts Christ. Therefore, it is a teaching that comes from the Spirit of God. When your heart is brought to rest upon what Christ has done, when, laying aside all confidence in your own works, knowledge, prayings, doings, or believings, you come to rest upon what Christ has done in its simplicity, then is Jesus Christ exalted in your heart. It must have been the work of the Spirit of divine grace. The person, then, and the work of Christ are exalted.

The Holy Spirit also exalts Christ in all His offices. That teaching that calls a man a priest and bids me take my child to receive some grace at his priestly hands and that puts another man into long sleeves and bids men kneel before him to receive a confirmation of his grace from his pretentious fingers, that system of religion that lifts up any one man above his fellowmen, as if there were any priests now except the common and general priesthood that belongs to every child of God—such teaching as that lowers Christ by lifting up human priests into Christ's place. The Spirit bears witness that Christ is the great High Priest of His church. It is from His hand we receive the blessing, through His blood we receive the washing, and nowhere else will we look for the grace that comes alone from Him.

Christ, too, is exalted by the Spirit in His prophetic, as well as in His priestly, office. Shall I call any man master so as to take him for my teacher? All teaching that lifts up Wesley or Calvin or any man, living or dead, in the place of the authorized Teacher, and that says that their dicta are to be taken as though they were the infallible revelations of Christ is not of the Spirit of God. But that teaching that says, "One is your Master, even Christ; and all ye are brethren" (Matt. 23:8), and that tells us of the holy equality of all saints and that the true, only Teacher who can speak with authority is Jesus Christ, the Son of God—such teaching you may accept as coming from God the Holy Spirit.

Then Christ occupies a third office—He is Prophet and Priest, and He is also King. Any teaching that puts Christ off the throne and puts someone else on is not according to the Spirit of God. The headship of Christ in His church is the doctrine that, perhaps beyond all others, needs to be taught at this time. It was for this that Scotland's sons suffered misery and death. Cast out, they wandered in the morasses and among the mountains. I stood the other day near the place where the monument is raised to thousands of men who had shed their blood for Christ. I felt it no small privilege to stand where Guthrie and others had poured out their blood for the defense of the headship of the church, when, forsooth, Charles II would be the head of the church, or James, or some other man of like character. But would this be tolerated by true-hearted saints of God's own true church? No; none but cravens and cowards will ever admit the authority of men or women over the church of Christ or permit them to usurp the rights divine of the Lord Jesus. When that day comes, when the King of Kings shall sit upon His throne, He will take summary vengeance upon the traitors who have dared to give up His high prerogatives. Christian, make Christ your Priest who absolves you; take Him as your only Leader and Prophet who is the truth and the life to you; then take Him as your King and bow your knee before Him; take Christ in all His offices to be exalted, for so the Spirit teaches.

Then Christ is also exalted by the Holy Spirit in His Word. There are some who think and say that they can do without the Bible, but such think and speak not by the Spirit of God, certainly. This is always an infallible test of the work of the Spirit, that He honors God's own Word. I could think no man true who, first of all, professed to write out his own mind and then afterward contradicted it. Then, how can that spirit be true that contradicts the writing of the Spirit of the living God? Bring whatever you have of revelation to the test of Scripture. If it accord not with that, throw it away. I wish this rule were learned by all men. Every now and then we read of or meet with persons who think that the Spirit has revealed to them something over and above what is in Scripture. Now, this is never the case. Any man who says that he has more revealed to him than is in the Holy Scripture incurs the curse of the last chapter of Revelation. He must take care lest, since he adds to the words of the Lord Jesus Christ, "God shall add unto him the plagues that are written in this book" (Rev. 22:18). "It is finished," must be said concerning this Book as we close it. Not a single verse or revelation shall henceforth come of the Spirit. Until Christ comes, this Book is sealed so far as any addition to it is concerned. It is not the Spirit of God that does not honor the Word of God.

Indeed, *there is nothing that concerns Christ that the Spirit of God does not magnify.* Consider any of His offices or His relationships, and you will find that the

Spirit magnifies and glorifies them, and so presents them to the believer's soul that he may rejoice therein.

Now, I advance a little further. The Holy Spirit's work is to glorify Christ, and *this He will do by filling you with Christ.* If you are subject to the work of the Spirit, then ought you to have much of the Spirit of Christ within you. But if you can live days and weeks without thinking of His person, set yourself down as being a hypocrite if you will, but you are not a true Christian. The very mark of the blessed man is that he lives upon God's Word. "In his law doth he meditate day and night" (Ps. 1:2). We feed upon Christ. As our bodies could not live without food, so neither can our souls live without Jesus. The Spirit of God will also fill your heart with Christ so that the more you have of that Spirit the more intense will be your love of the Savior until at last you will be able to say—

> Jesus the very thought of thee
> With sweetness fills my breast.

When the Spirit of God is with you, you will feel indeed that it is so. No joy can be compared with that of the love of Christ shed abroad in your heart. When the Spirit has thus filled your thoughts and hearts, He will be sure to occupy your tongues. They who love the Savior must speak of Him. In choice company, they will tell some of the secrets of His love, and in any company they will not be ashamed to own that they are His servants. Occupying the tongue, He will be sure also to engage it in prayer for Him, and they will not cease to offer such prayers as these: "Thy kingdom come. Jesus, be thou exalted. Oh, when will you come, in thy chariot of salvation, to ride over the whole earth? Come quickly, come quickly, Lord Jesus!" And then, too, your tongue will be employed in songs concerning Him. It is always a token of a revival of religion, it is said, when there is a revival of psalmody. When Luther's preaching began to tell upon men, you could hear plowmen at the plow-tail singing Luther's psalms. Whitefield and Wesley would never have done the great work they did if it had not been for Charles Wesley's poetry and for the singing of such men as Toplady and Scott and Newton and many others of the same class. Even now we mark that since there has been somewhat of a religious revival in our various denominations, there are more hymnbooks than ever there were before, and far more attention is paid to Christian psalmody than ever before. When your heart is full of Christ, you will want to sing. It is a blessed thing to sing at your labor and work if you are in a place where you can do so. If the world should laugh at you, you must tell them that you have as good a right to sing the songs that delight your heart as they have to sing any of the songs in which their hearts delight. Praise His name, Christians. Be not dumb; sing aloud to Jesus the Lamb. If we as Englishmen can sometimes sing our national air, let us as believers have our national hymn, and sing—

> Crown him, crown him,
> Crown him Lord of all.

And, surely, when the Spirit of God thus honors Christ in the tongue, it will not stop there. It comes to the acts of daily life. *The Spirit shall glorify Christ by helping you to glorify Him in your own actions.* I spoke this morning of some who set themselves apart for extraordinary service. I did not, however, intend to imply that that was at all necessary, for you may serve Christ as good housewives, you may serve Him as merchants, shopkeepers, and, in short, in every condition of life. Our religion is for the marketplace, for the shop, for the streets, and for the field. And as God's being is not confined to temples made by the hands of men, but is present everywhere, on heath and city and moor and field—in the sunbeams that light the peasant's cot as well as the monarch's palace, present in the minute as well as in the magnificent, down there in the glades where the red deer wander and the child loves to play and up there where the storms gather upon the mountain's hoary brow, as visible in a blade of grass as in the cedar and the tall waving pine, to be seen as well in the dewdrop as in the avalanche, as certainly in the falling of a leaf as in the tremendous roar of the thunder—everywhere present, so is true religion everywhere, in the cottage as well as in the temple, in business as well as in devotions, abroad in the streets as well as in the silence of retirement, up yonder where men wrestle with God, and down there where they come to contend with men and for His truth. You have never received the Spirit so as to know that Christ is the glorified One unless in your life as well as with your lips you do show forth His praise.

If the Spirit has thus far instructed you, He will conduct you a little further, and you may accept His teaching because it glorifies Christ. There are some doctrines that are not often preached in certain pulpits; they are supposed to be rather dangerous. Speaking of a certain hymnbook, I remarked to a minister in whose pulpit I preached that I did not like the hymnbook as I could never find a hymn that sang of the covenant of grace or the doctrine of election. "Oh, well," he said, "that is no disadvantage to me, for I never say anything about those doctrines"; and I can quite believe what he said. There are certain higher truths that only belong to those who have passed through the rudiments and have done with the grammar school book and can enter into the university. One of the things that glorifies Christ is when the Spirit makes us understand the eternal love of Christ to His people and His covenant engagements for them.

Christian, I would have you know that Christ never did begin to love you! Before the mountains were piled, or the clouds had gathered about them, Christ had set His heart upon you. No, when this great world and the sun and moon and stars slept in the mind of God like forests in an acorn cup, then, then had Jehovah-Jesus love for you. And when the proper time came, He offered Himself up as a Surety for your soul, to pay your debts, to stand as your Representative, to keep you in this world, and to present you at the last to the Father as a priceless jewel. Oh, how you will glorify Christ if you have faith enough to take in this divine mystery! Stagger not at electing love; it is one of the highest notes of heavenly music. Be not afraid of such a verse as this: "I have loved thee with an everlasting love: therefore with lovingkindness have I drawn thee" (Jer. 31:3). Here is marrow and fatness such as saints fed upon in days long since gone.

Take another truth, the precious truth of the *finished* work of Christ for His people. How often do you hear Christ's work preached as if it were only begun. Many hold Him up as though He had commenced a fitting garment, but had left off somewhere so that by adding our rags we might complete the work. I was in one of the vaults of the British Museum some time since, when the sculptures came from Nineveh, and one of them was unfinished. There was evidently the last mark that the mason had made before he was destroyed, or, it may be, called away from his work to which he never returned. But Jesus Christ has left no sculpture of this kind; He has finished all His work. "It is finished" (John 19:30, etc.) were words that gladdened earth and made heaven more glorious. There is nothing now for souls to do to save themselves. For whom Jesus died that soul is saved. All that soul has to do is, being saved, to show its gratitude and love as one that is brought to life from the dead.

> Loved of my God, for him again
> With love intense I burn;
> Chosen of him ere time began,
> I chose him in return.

You may know that perfection in Christ by a firm reliance upon the Scriptures. How can you perish? You are saved; there is, therefore, now no condemnation recorded against you. Who shall lay anything to your charge? Who shall separate you from the love of God that is in Christ Jesus your Lord?

If there is one doctrine, however, more sweet and

yet more deep than another, it is the divine doctrine of that eternal union which exists between Christ and His people. It is the Spirit's work to take the golden key and let us into this secret cabinet. Believers are one with Christ; by vital personal union they are one with Him. They are members of His body, or as He Himself says, they are the branches, and He is the Vine; they are the members, and He is the Head. I know of nothing that can be more delightful than this union—this eternal union—with Christ.

> One in the tomb, one when he rose,
> One when he triumphed o'er his foes,
> One when in heaven he took his seat,
> While seraphs sang all hell's defeat.

> This sacred tie forbids our fears;
> For all he is or has is ours;
> With him, our Head, we stand or fall,
> Our life, our surety, and our all.

It used to be said, by an excellent theologian, that any man who understood the two covenants of works and grace was a master in theology. Yet, oh, how few Christians there seem to be who really understand the covenant of grace! "As in Adam all die, even so in Christ shall all be made alive" (1 Cor. 15:22). We fell, not by our own fault, but by Adam's fault; we rise, not by our own virtue, but by virtue of our union with Christ. If you are in Christ, believer, you are safe while Christ stands. You cannot drown the body until you drown the Head. My foot may be deep in the stream, but until the billows roll over my brow, my foot is not drowned. Until Christ shall perish, no soul that is one with Christ can be destroyed. He said to His disciples, "Because I live, ye shall live also" (John 14:19). Did time permit, I might enter into some more of those sublime mysteries that make the core and pith of the comfort of the Christian, but I forbear. May the Spirit of God glorify Christ by taking these things of Christ and revealing them to you and making them personally yours!

And to close—the Holy Spirit will continue all your life, if you are a believer in Christ, to further His work in you *by writing all that concerns Christ upon your experience and your life.* I long to see in the church more men and women who have Christ so glorified in them that their faith never staggers, who have neither doubts nor fears, who know whom they have believed, who are persuaded that He is able to keep that which they have committed to Him, who leave all things to the Father's wisdom and find everything in a perfect Savior. I long to see some of you made partakers of our overflowing joy. I long to see your eyes flash with the joyous radiance of your Savior's presence. I pray that you may be so full of joy that when you speak you may cheer the downcast and lift up the countenances of the sad. I want you to have added to this an intense and fervent love—love that shall perform impossibilities, that shall dare anything for Christ—that, impelled by zeal, shall thresh the mountains and beat them small, and shall winnow the wheat from the chaff upon the threshing floor. I pray that you may have that mighty consecration of spirit that shall make you altogether unearthly, that as you have borne the image of the earthy, you may also bear the image of the heavenly. As you have been conformed to the first Adam in the curse, and in all the infirmities and griefs of this mortal life, you may be conformed to the second Adam in His pure unselfish love for man, His noble, all-daring, all-consuming love for His Father and for His cause.

I am persuaded that the Spirit does not glorify Christ in us so much as He would if we gave ourselves up more fully to the Savior. As one said on a certain occasion, there is a fleet lying in the river, richly-laden, but it cannot come up because the river is blocked up with ice. So, I think, I see my Master's love lying out far down the river, and it would fain come to my poor soul to enrich me and make me holy and heavenly. But, alas! the coldness of my heart, like ice, blocks up the channel and I get not what I might obtain. Come, heavenly love, and melt the ice; flow, streams of grace, and dissolve every barrier; come Jesus, come into my heart, and let Your treasures be mine forevermore! Oh, that I could stir some believers here to seek more than is generally enjoyed by Christians! May God give you the seraphic earnestness of a Whitefield, the deep piety of a Martyn, the lovely spirit of a Newton or a Cowper! May He fill you to the brim with Himself until you shall be like a city set upon a hill that cannot be hid, and like to candles in the house that enlighten all around!

But, alas! there are some here who know not my Master at all, who are strangers to His love. There is Christ looking down upon you with tearful eye, and He bids you come to Him. That blood which you have hitherto despised will wash away your every sin. Only cast yourself upon Him. Look up into those languid eyes, for they are full of pity yet. That streaming blood flows to every soul that trusts in Jesus. Read the mystery of that pierced heart; there is love alone written there. Study the anguish of that poor martyred body, for in every pang you can learn the story of His compassion. As you see Him bowing His head and hear Him saying, "Father, into thy hands I commend my spirit" (Luke 23:46), He asks you, every one, to commend your spirit to Him. Do it, do it now, God helping you, and Christ will thus be glorified.

Is the Spirit of the Lord Straitened?

Alexander Maclaren (1826–1910) was one of Great Britain's most famous preachers. While pastoring the Union Chapel, Manchester (1858–1903), he became known as "the prince of expository preachers." Rarely active in denominational or civic affairs, Maclaren invested his time in studying the Word in the original languages and sharing its truths with others in sermons that are still models of effective expository preaching. He published a number of books of sermons and climaxed his ministry by publishing his monumental *Expositions of Holy Scripture*.

This message is taken from *Christ in the Heart*, published in 1902 by Funk and Wagnalls, New York.

Alexander Maclaren

4
IS THE SPIRIT OF THE LORD STRAITENED?

O thou that art named the house of Jacob, is the Spirit of the LORD straitened? are these his doings? (Micah 2:7).

THE GREATER PART OF so-called Christendom is today celebrating the gift of a Divine Spirit to the church, but it may well be asked whether the religious condition of so-called Christendom is not a sad satire upon Pentecost. There seems a woeful contrast, very perplexing to faith, between the bright promise at the beginning and the history of the development in the future. How few of those who share in today's services have any personal experience of such a gift! How many seem to think that that old story is only the record of a past event, a transient miracle that has no kind of relation to the experience of the Christians of this day! There were a handful of believers in one of the towns of Asia Minor to whom an apostle came and was so startled at their condition that he put to them in wonder the question that might well be put to multitudes of so-called Christians among us: "Did ye receive the Holy Ghost when ye believed?" (Acts 19:2 RV). And their answer is only too true a transcript of the experience of large masses of people who call themselves Christians: "We have not so much as heard whether there be any Holy Ghost."

I desire, then, friends to avail myself of this day's associations in order to press upon your consciences and upon my own some considerations naturally suggested by them, and that find voice in these two indignant questions of the old prophet: "Is the Spirit of the LORD straitened?" Are these the phenomena of existing popular Christianity—"are these his doings?" And if we are brought sharp up against the consciousness of a dreadful contrast, it may do us good to ask what is the explanation of so cloudy a day following a morning so bright.

The Promise of the Pentecost

What did the promise of Pentecost declare and hold forth for the faith of the church? I need not dwell at any length upon this point. The facts are familiar to you, and the inferences drawn from them are commonplace and known to us all. But let me just enumerate them as briefly as may be.

"Suddenly there came a sound . . . as of a rushing mighty wind, and it filled all the house where they were sitting. And there appeared . . . cloven tongues like as of fire, and it sat upon each of them. And they were all filled with the Holy Ghost" (Acts 2:2).

What lay in that? First, the promise of a Divine Spirit by symbols that express some, at all events, of the characteristics and wonderfulness of His work. The rushing of a mighty wind spoke of a power that varies in its manifestations from the gentlest breath, which scarce moves the leaves on the summer trees, to the wildest blast, which casts down all that stands in its way.

The natural symbolism of the wind, the least material of all material forces, in connection with the immaterial of a man's personality has been expressed in all languages. It points to a Divine, to an immaterial, to a mighty, to a life-giving power that is free to blow whither it listeth, of which men can mark the effects, though they are all ignorant of the force itself.

The twin symbol of the fiery tongues which parted and sat upon each of them speaks in like manner of the Divine influence, not as destructive, but full of quick, rejoicing energy and life, the power to transform and to purify. Whithersoever the fire comes, it changes all things into its own substance. Whithersoever the fire comes, there the ruddy spires shoot upward toward the heavens.

Maclaren: *Is the Spirit of the Lord Straitened?* / 55

Whithersoever the fire comes, there all bonds and fetters are melted and consumed. And so this fire transforms, purifies, ennobles, quickens, sets free; where the fiery Spirit is, there is energy, swift life, rejoicing activity, transforming and transmuting power which changes the recipient of the flame into flame himself.

Then, still further, in the fact of Pentecost there is the promise of a Divine Spirit that is to influence all the moral side of humanity. This is the great and glorious distinction between the Christian doctrine of inspiration and all others that have, in heathen lands, partially reached similar conceptions—that the Gospel of Jesus Christ has laid emphasis upon the *Holy* Spirit, and has declared that holiness of heart is the touchstone and test of all claims of divine inspiration. Gifts are much, graces are more. An inspiration that makes wise is to be coveted, an inspiration that makes holy is transcendently better. There we find the safeguard against all the fanaticisms that have sometimes invaded the Christian church, namely, in the thought that the Spirit, which dwells in men and makes them free from the obligations of outward law and cold morality, is a Spirit that works a deeper holiness than law dreamed, and a more spontaneous and glad conformity to all things that are fair and good than any legislation and outward commandment could ever enforce. The Spirit that came at Pentecost is not merely a Spirit of rushing might and of swift-flaming energy, but it is a Spirit of holiness, whose most blessed and intimate work is the production in us of all the homely virtues and sweet, unpretending goodnesses which adorn and gladden humanity.

Still further, the Pentecost carried in it the promise and prophecy of a Spirit granted to all the church. "They were all filled with the Holy Ghost." This is the true democracy of Christianity, that its very basis is laid in the thought that every member of the body is equally close to the Head and equally recipient of the life. There are none now who have a Spirit that others do not possess. The ancient aspiration of the Jewish lawgiver: "Would God that all the LORD's people were prophets, and that the LORD would put his spirit upon them" (Num. 11:29), is fulfilled in the experience of Pentecost; the attendant and the children, as well as the old men and the servants, receive of that universal gift. Therefore sacerdotal claims, special functions, privileged classes, are alien to the spirit of Christianity, and blasphemies against the inspiring God. If "one is your master, . . . all ye are brethren" (Matt. 23:8). And if we have all been made to drink into one Spirit, then no longer has any man dominion over our faith nor power to intervene and to intercede with God for us.

And still further, the promise of the early history was that of a Spirit that should fill the whole nature of those to whom He was granted; filling, in the measure, of course, of their receptivity, filling them as the great sea does all the creeks and indentations along the shore. The deeper the creek, the deeper the water in it. The further inland it runs, the further will the refreshing tide penetrate the bosom of the continent. And so each one, according to character, stature, circumstances, and all the varying conditions that determine power of receptivity, will receive a varying measure of that gift. Yet it is meant that all shall be full. The little vessel, the tiny cup, as well as the great cistern and the enormous vat, each contains according to its capacity. And if all are filled, then this quick Spirit must have the power to influence all the provinces of human nature, must touch the moral, must touch the spiritual. The temporary manifestations and extraordinary signs of His power may well drop away as the flower drops when the fruit has set. The operations of the Divine Spirit are to be felt thrilling through all the nature, and every part of the man's being is to be recipient of the power. Just as when you take a candle and plunge it into a jar of oxygen it blazes up, so my poor human nature immersed in that Divine Spirit, baptized in the Holy Spirit, shall flame in all its parts into unsuspected and hitherto inexperienced brightness. Such are the elements of the promise of Pentecost.

The Apparent Failure of the Promise

"Is the Spirit of the LORD straitened?" Look at Christendom. Look at all the churches. Look at yourselves. Will anyone say that the religious condition of any body of professed believers at this moment corresponds to Pentecost? Is not the gap so wide that to fill it up seems almost impossible? Is not the stained and imperfect fulfillment a miserable satire upon the promise? "If the LORD be with us," said one of the heroes of ancient Israel, "why then is all this befallen us?" (Judg. 6:13). And I am sure that we may say the same. If the Lord be with us, what is the meaning of the state of things that we see around us and must recognize in ourselves? Do any existing churches present the final perfect form of Christianity as embodied in a society? Would not the best thing that could happen, and the thing that will have to happen some day, be the disintegration of the existing organizations in order to build up a more perfect habitation of God through the Spirit? I do not want to exaggerate. God knows there is no need for exaggerating. The plain, unvarnished story, without any pessimistic picking out of the black bits and forgetting all the light ones, is bad enough.

Take three points on which I do not dwell and apply them to yourselves, dear friends, and estimate by them the condition of things around us. First, say whether the ordinary tenor of our own religious life looks as if we had that Divine Spirit in us that transforms everything into its own beauty, and makes men, through all the regions of their natures, holy and pure. Then ask yourselves the question whether the standard of devotion and consecration in any church witnesses of the presence of a Divine Spirit. A little handful of people, the best of them very partially touched with the life of God, and very imperfectly consecrated to His service, surrounded by a great mass about whom we can scarcely, in the judgment of charity, say even so much—that is the description of most of our congregations. Are these His doings? Surely somebody else's than His.

Take another question. Do the relations of modern Christians and their churches to one another attest the presence of a unifying Spirit? We "have been all made to drink into one Spirit" (1 Cor. 12:13), said Paul. Alas! Alas, does it seem as if we had? Look round professing Christendom, look at the rivalries and the jealousies between two chapels in adjoining streets. Look at the gulfs between Christian men who differ only on some comparative trifle of organization and polity and say if such things correspond to the Pentecostal promise of one Spirit that is to make all the members into one body? Is the Spirit of the Lord straitened? Are these *His* doings?

Take another branch of evidence. Look at the comparative impotence of the church in its conflict with the growing worldliness of the world. I do not forget how much is being done all about us today and how still Christ's Gospel is winning triumphs. Look thoughtfully and dispassionately on the condition say, for instance, of Manchester or of any of our great towns; mark how the populace knows nothing and cares nothing about us and our Christianity and never comes into our places of worship and has no share in our hopes any more than if they lived in central Africa—and that is so after eighteen hundred years of nominal Christianity. Can you look without feeling that some malign influence has arrested the leaping growth of the early church and that somehow or other that lava stream, if I might so call it, which poured hot from the heart of God in the old day, has had its flow checked, and over its burning bed there has spread a black and wrinkled crust, whatsoever lingering heat there may still be at the center? If God be with us, why has all this come upon us?

The Solution of the Contradiction

The indignant questions of my text may be taken, with a little possibly permissible violence, as expressing and dismissing some untrue explanations. One explanation that sometimes is urged is that the Spirit of the

Lord *is* straitened. That explanation takes two forms. Sometimes you hear people saying, "Christianity is effete. We have to go now to fresh fountains of inspiration and turn away from these broken cisterns that can hold no water." I am not going to argue that question. I do not think for my part that Christianity will be effete until the world has got up to it and beyond it in its practice, and it will be a good while before that happens. Christianity will not be worn out until men have copied and reduced to practice the example of Jesus Christ, and they have not quite got that length yet. No shadow of a fear that the Gospel has lost its power or that God's Spirit has become weak should be permitted to creep over our hearts. The promise is, "I will pray the Father, and he shall give you another Comforter, that he may abide with you for ever" (John 14:16). It is a permanent gift that was given to the church on that day. We have to distinguish in the story between the symbols, the gift, and the consequences of the gift. The first and the last are transient, the second is permanent. The symbols were transient. The people that gathered together saw no tongues of fire. The consequences were transient. The tongues and the miraculous utterances were but for a time. The results vary according to the circumstances. But the central thing, the gift itself, is an irrevocable gift and, once bestowed, is ever with the church to all generations.

Another form of the explanation is the theory that God in His sovereignty is pleased to withhold His Spirit for reasons that we cannot trace. But it is not true that the gift once given varies in the degree in which it is continued. There is always the same flow from God. There are ebbs and flows in the spiritual power of the church. Yes! And the tide runs out of your harbors. Is there any less water in the sea because it does? So the gift may ebb away from a man, from a community, from an epoch, not because God's manifestation and bestowment fluctuates, but because our receptivity changes. So we dismiss, and are bound to dismiss, if we are Christians, the unbelieving explanation that the Spirit of the Lord is straitened, and we do not sit with our hands folded, as if an inscrutable sovereignty, with which we have nothing to do, sometimes sent more and sometimes less of His spiritual gifts upon a waiting church. It is not so. With Him is no variableness. The gifts of God are without repentance and the Spirit that was given once, according to the Master's own word already quoted, is given that He may abide with us forever.

Therefore we have to come back to this, which is the point to which I seek to bring you and myself in lowly penitence and contrite acknowledgment—that it is all our own fault and the result of evil in ourselves that may be remedied that we have so little of that divine gift. If the churches of this country and of this day seem to be cursed and blasted in so much of their fruitless operations and formal worship, it is the fault of the churches and not of the Lord of the churches. The stream that poured forth from the throne of God has not lost itself in the sands, nor is it shrunken in its volume. The fire that was kindled on Pentecost has not died down into gray ashes. The rushing of the mighty wind that woke on that morning has not calmed and stilled itself into the stagnancy and suffocating breathlessness of midday heat. The same fullness of the Spirit which filled the believers on that day is available for us all. If, like that waiting church of old, we abide in prayer and supplication, the gift will be given to us too. We may repeat and reproduce, if not the miracles which we do not need, yet the necessary inspiration of the highest and the noblest days and saints in the history of the church. "If ye then, being evil, know how unto give good gifts to your children: how much more shall your heavenly Father give the Holy Spirit to them that ask him?" (Luke 11:13). Ask, and you shall receive and be filled with the Holy Spirit and with power.

NOTES

Belated Saints

Clovis Gillham Chappell (1882–1972) was one of American Methodism's best-known and most effective preachers. He pastored churches in Washington, D.C.; Dallas and Houston, Texas; Memphis, Tennessee; and Birmingham, Alabama; and his pulpit ministry drew great crowds. He was especially known for his biographical sermons that made biblical figures live and speak to our modern day. He published about thirty volumes of sermons.

This message was taken from *Chappell's Special Day Sermons*, reprinted in 1976 by Baker Book House.

Clovis Gillham Chappell

5
BELATED SAINTS

All the baptism he knew was that of John (Acts 18:25 MOFFATT).

"ALL THE BAPTISM HE knew was that of John." That is a rather surprising and startling statement to read of one who has been instructed in the things of the Lord. It becomes even more so when we realize that the one so instructed has accepted that instruction and has actually become a disciple of Jesus. And, while the spiritual requirements for the pulpit are no greater than those for the pew, it becomes more surprising still when we realize that this man has not only become a disciple, but has entered the Christian ministry. Yet, such is the case. Apollos is a preacher. He is one of the great men of the early church. He has set himself to the tremendous task of remaking men and of bringing in the kingdom of God. But, sad to say, he undertakes this amazing impossibility knowing only the baptism of John. What inadequate equipment! How can he hope for anything better than heartbreaking failure? He has much, but he does not have enough.

Look at the Wealth of His Equipment

He is a man of great native gifts. Now, we are not forgetting the fact that the bulk of the world's work must be done by us who are of mediocre ability. Nor are we forgetting that the man of one talent is just as worthy of honor as the man that has five. No man is to be crowned simply because he is gifted. Large gifts do not reflect credit upon the receiver, but upon the giver. But while this is true, it is also true that vast ability opens the door to vast usefulness. A consecrated million will surely do more than a consecrated penny.

Therefore, we are glad to welcome into our brotherhood this man of outstanding ability. And we rejoice that through the centuries so many of the world's greatest intellects have consecrated their large gifts to the service of the kingdom.

He is a man of fine culture. He is a native of Alexandria. This city, like the native city of Saint Paul, was the seat of a university. It also possessed the greatest library of antiquity. It was a city of scholars and philosophers. Apollos has, therefore, been exposed to the finest educational opportunities of his day. Not only so, but he has made wise use of those opportunities. Thus he has brought to the work of the ministry one of the best-trained minds of his day. So splendidly equipped is he both by nature and training that he is able to preach even in the pulpit of the marvelously endowed and cultured Paul. In fact Paul has to share honors with him. And no wonder. Such a preacher would be capable of winning a hearing in any age. In fact, Apollos, Paul, and Luke share the honor of being the three best-trained men of the early church.

He is a man of flaming zeal. He has kept the hot fires of a fine enthusiasm burning upon the altar of his soul. That is splendid. The truly worthwhile work of this world is ever done by the hot-hearted. It is these, too, who call out the best there is in us. The tepid, timid, halfhearted individual does little and makes little appeal to either God or man. And the burning ardor of Apollos is all the more dynamic because it is coupled with high culture. Unfortunately, outstanding scholarship and flaming zeal do not always walk arm in arm. There are those the chief ends of whose learning seem to be either to serve as a new kind of fire extinguisher or for cold storage purposes. Of course, this is not the fault of scholarship. Certainly we are not to conclude that the fine flower of zeal thrives only in the lean soil of ignorance. We have all known men like Apollos who were at once highly cultured and highly zealous. We have all known also those who were at once dreadfully lacking both in knowledge and also in zeal. Hot enthusiasm is good in any worthy cause, but the more intelligent it is, the better. Therefore, we appreciate especially the zeal of Apollos.

He is mighty in the Scriptures. How refreshing! No disciple who aspires to a vigorous spiritual life can afford to neglect the Bible. Certainly no one who teaches in the church school or holds a position of leadership in the church can afford to slight this supreme book of mankind. But the Bible is the preacher's specialty. He is expected to be able to teach it with some degree of assurance and authority. Apollos has studied and read widely, but he has majored on the Word of God. Therefore, Luke could write of him that he was mighty in the Scriptures. We congratulate him and we congratulate those who were privileged to sit under his ministry. It is well for the preacher to be mighty in organization, mighty in financiering, but it is better still for him to be mighty in the Scriptures. It is such men whose ministry has ever been most rich in abiding usefulness. Bunyan has guided millions toward the Celestial City. This he has done, not simply because he was a genius at allegory, but more still because he was mighty in the Scriptures.

He is hospitable to the truth. He is eager and ready to learn from anyone who is able and willing to teach. That is his salvation. That is what kept him from squandering his fine resources for returns meager in quantity and poor in quality. Being eager to learn, he is, therefore, capable of teaching and preaching. To close the door of the mind is fatal. Years ago I knew a young man of high possibilities who decided to enter the ministry. His educational opportunities were of the very best. His work both in college and seminary was full of promise. But having finished his training and entered upon his chosen work, he seemed to think that his days of toil were over. He quit reading. He quit growing. He became a victim of arrested development, a disappointment to himself and to others.

Apollos is different. He is possessed of an eager mind and heart. He continues to learn and, therefore, to grow.

And what is more commendable still, he is willing to learn about his own specialty, and that from those who were doubtless far his inferiors both in ability and culture. Surely a rare man is Apollos. Were I serving on the committee for securing a new pastor for my church, I should give careful consideration to this gifted, cultured, zealous, open-minded, and scriptural preacher. But having considered, I greatly fear I should have to vote against him. This is true because Apollos has one great defect that, if left uncorrected, must cause his brilliant ministry to be little better than a failure.

What Is Wrong with Apollos?

What is wrong with Apollos? It is not that he is a heretic. No more is he a wild and foolish fanatic. He has not been improperly instructed; he has been inadequately instructed. All the baptism he knows is that of John. He does not know the baptism of the Holy Spirit. He has not entered into that life-giving, transforming experience that came to his fellow disciples at Pentecost. He is thus belated, completely behind the times spiritually. He simply has not arrived. He is not in reality a Christian at all. Therefore, in spite of all his lordly gifts, in spite of his commendable zeal, he is but poorly equipped for the great work to which he has set his hand. No man is adequate for the task of Christian living and of kingdom building whose adequacy is not of the Holy Spirit.

This is the plain teaching of our Lord. "It is the spirit that quickeneth" (John 6:63). How well fitted were Peter and John after they had seen their risen Lord! They had companied with Him during the days of His earthly ministry. They had seen Him die. They had seen His tomb, which was at the same time the grave of their dearest hopes. Peter had looked upon this grave with increased bitterness because of his cowardly denial of Him. But a new day has dawned. It is Easter Sunday. Christ has risen—the same forgiving Savior as of old. He can hardly wait to get the door of the tomb open before He sends a special message to

Peter and grants him a private interview. Thus the past is buried, and Peter has a wonderful story to tell. His fellow disciples share his message and passion. But Jesus says, Not yet. Wait for the promise of the Father. "Tarry ye . . . until ye be endued with power from on high" (Luke 24:49).

And just as it is true that no man is adequate without this experience that Apollos lacked, it is equally true that to all who claim it there comes an amazing adequacy. We think wistfully at times of the privilege of those early friends of Jesus. How wonderful to have walked by His side, to have felt the touch of His hand, to have sat under the spell of His voice! No wonder that their hearts were crushed when they found that He was going to leave them. No wonder that they could not think of the empty, gray days ahead without their faces being wet by hot and bitter tears. But Jesus tells them, in His quiet way, that by going He is doing the best possible for them. "It is expedient for you that I go away" (John 16:7)—My going is the roadway to an infinite nearness. And, incredible as it seemed, they find it gloriously true. They realize after Pentecost that He is not only with them, but within them. He is now more blessedly near and real than ever before.

"All the baptism he knew was that of John." What a fatal defect, what a tragic loss! For this means that though he knows about Jesus, he does not know Jesus Himself. He knows about Him, but he does not realize Him. He cannot say with Paul, "Have I not seen Jesus Christ our Lord?" (1 Cor. 9:1). He cannot shout with him with unshaken and unshakable conviction, "I know whom I have believed, and am persuaded that he is able to keep that which I have committed unto him against that day" (2 Tim. 1:12). He has, therefore, missed the one supreme essential of Christianity. Knowing only the baptism of John, the Spirit is not yet able to take the things of Christ and to show them to him.

Being unable to realize Christ, he is alike unable to reproduce Him. He has not become a new creation. He cannot say with the Spirit-baptized, "For me to live is

Christ" (Phil. 1:21). He cannot sing, "I am crucified with Christ: nevertheless I live; yet not I, but Christ liveth in me" (Gal. 2:20). Men do not take knowledge of him that he has been with Jesus. Lacking the Spirit, though he seeks to imitate Christ, he cannot incarnate Him. Like so many today, he is simply undertaking to do in the energy of the flesh what can only be done in the power of the Spirit.

Of course, this sad defect tells upon his entire ministry. It tells upon his personal contacts and upon his preaching. He is an eloquent and forceful speaker. Those who hear him are instructed. They are doubtless thrilled and entertained. They are compelled to admire his many fine qualities. But in spite of all this, he somehow fails to bring them a sense of the presence of Christ. He does not compel them to say in their hushed and awed hearts, "Surely, God is in this place." Therefore, though a wonderfully attractive preacher, he is not a powerful preacher. Though eloquent and earnest, he is not greatly helpful.

It is evident that those choice saints Aquila and Priscilla are disappointed in him. They have doubtless looked with eager anticipation to his coming to Ephesus. Now that he has come, they go to the service with high expectancy. But the preacher has hardly begun before they feel that there is something lacking, and they are very sure what that something is. They realize sadly that in his ministry to the saints this great preacher is little better than a failure. Nor does he seem to be more successful with those outside the church. We have no right to say, of course, that those twelve backward disciples that Paul found upon his visit to Ephesus were converts of Apollos. But this, at least, we may say: They are the kind of converts we should expect him to make. They are like him in their entire ignorance of the baptism of the Holy Spirit.

Now, many years have passed since then, years in which Christianity has spread around the world. But after all these centuries, we cannot shut our eyes to the fact that there are vast numbers in the church today that are just as far behind the times as Apollos. In fact I am afraid that this distinguished minister would feel far more at home among a group of modern saints than among those of whom he was a part. It is my very firm conviction that the saddest lack of the church today is that from which Apollos was suffering. We need his ability and culture, but there must be something more. If I were asked to point out the greatest weakness of the pew today, I should have to say a lack of a vital religious experience. If I should be asked to indicate the greatest weakness of our increasingly efficient teaching force, I should have to give the same answer. If I should be asked the same question with regard to our ministry, which is the best-trained the church has ever had, I should have to give the same monotonous answer. Therefore, many of us are tired and harassed and discouraged. This is true because we insist upon undertaking in the energy of the flesh what we can only do in the power of the Spirit.

Is There a Way Out for Apollos?

Is there a way out for Apollos? Is there a way out for ourselves? I am perfectly sure that we may answer in the affirmative.

Look at Apollos. He preaches the best he can, but is disappointing. When the service is over Aquila and Priscilla do not pass the word along that the preacher is unsafe and that they had better refuse to give him any further hearing. Had they done so they might have worked a great injury both to the preacher and to the congregation. Instead they do that which indicates both consecration and tact of the highest order. They doubtless invite the preacher home with them for dinner. The meal over, they proceed to expound to him the way of the Lord more perfectly. That is magnificent. It is hard to tell which to admire the more, the instructors or the instructed. It is certainly a delicate matter to instruct a preacher, for we are a sensitive tribe. Great credit is due these tactful teachers. But great credit is also due Apollos. He does not flash his diploma and his various degrees at them. Instead he listens with childlike humility. As he listens, his heart burns within him. He feels that here is good news indeed.

What, I wonder, do they say to this earnest man who is working so hard and doing so little? I think they tell him what has recently taken place at Pentecost. They tell him that Jesus who was so accessible to His friends in the days of His flesh is far more accessible now, that He has come again in the person of the Holy Spirit, and that He now offers Himself to every man who will receive Him. "This," they add, "is not mere theory. It is a fact of experience. We have tested it and found it true. We are finding it true even now. He is with us day by day and hour by hour as a living reality."

And is not this just the message that you and I need? Being religious is such a chore for many of us. We often feel that in spite of all our wearying efforts we have made a bit of a mess of it. In our efforts to be like Christ we feel that we have been about as successful as if we had been out seeking that fabled pot of gold at the end of the rainbow. The nimble goddess of the mists has fled far faster than we could pursue. All that we seem to have won is torn garments, sore feet, and a yet sorer heart. What is wrong? How have we missed the way? Maybe our mistake has been that of Simon Magus. He thought that this gift might be purchased. Of course we have not offered vulgar coin as he did. We have, rather, offered other values like earnest effort, a correct creed, strict orthodoxy. Or perchance, as Apollos, we have failed to hear the news, and are simply spiritually behind the times.

What, then, we need to know is that the Spirit has indeed been given, and that He is not a blessing to be bought, but a gift to be received. "*Receive* ye" (John 20:22), said Jesus as He breathed upon His disciples in the long ago. So He is saying still. This is the very heart of the Gospel. In fact it is exactly what makes a gospel of the Christian message. Jesus does not have to be coaxed into our lives. He has only, in the personality of the Holy Spirit, to be received. The whole New Testament fairly haunts us with this truth. "This spake he of the Spirit, which they that believe on him were to receive." They "have *received* the Holy Ghost as well as we" (Acts 10:47). "Then laid they their hands on them, and they received the Holy Ghost" (Acts 8:17). And hearing this good news, Apollos believes and receives. The same rich privilege is ours also. "For the promise is unto you, and to your children, and to all that are afar off, even as many as the Lord our God shall call" (Acts 2:39).

We do not know as much about Apollos after this experience as we should like. But of this we may be sure, that his ministry took on a new joy and a new power. When we catch a glimpse of him in Corinth a little later we read this of him: He "helped them much" (Acts 18:27). What a revealing word! When he was behind the times they spoke of him as a learned, zealous, and eloquent preacher. Now he is a helpful preacher. That is infinitely better. And the sweet wonder of it is that this is a type of ministry that is open to every one of us, whether we preach from pulpit or pew. We cannot all be learned and eloquent, but by sharing this experience of Apollos we can all be helpful. This is the sure word of Jesus Himself. "If any man thirst, let him come unto me, and drink. He that believeth on me, as the scripture hath said, out of his [inner life] shall flow rivers of living water" (John 7:37).

The Holy Spirit through Christ, in the Church, for the World

George Campbell Morgan (1863–1945) was the son of a British Baptist preacher and preached his first sermon when he was thirteen years old. He had no formal training for the ministry, but his tireless devotion to the study of the Bible helped him to become one of the leading Bible teachers of his day. Rejected by the Methodists, he was ordained into the Congregational ministry. He was associated with Dwight L. Moody in the Northfield Bible conferences and as an itinerant Bible teacher. He is best known as the pastor of the Westminster Chapel, London (1904–1917 and 1933–1945). During his second term there, he had Dr. D. Martyn Lloyd-Jones as his associate.

Morgan published more than sixty books and booklets, and his sermons are found in *The Westminster Pulpit* (Hodder and Stoughton). This sermon is from volume 6.

G. Campbell Morgan

6

THE HOLY SPIRIT THROUGH CHRIST, IN THE CHURCH, FOR THE WORLD

> Being therefore by the right hand of God exalted, and having received of the Father the promise of the Holy Ghost, he hath poured forth this, which ye see and hear (Acts 2:33 RV).

CHRISTIANITY'S SUPREME CREDENTIAL IS Christianity. Of all miracles it is the greatest. There are two historic facts that are indisputable: first, the death of Jesus, and, second, the church of Jesus. Or to put that in another way, history attests the fact that somehow or other out of death came life, that after the death of Jesus there began in human history a new order of men and women, a new order of society, new ideals, new impulses, new forces. That is the supreme wonder. We look back again to the Cross of our Lord, and we may say of Him reverently, in the language of the writer of the letter to the Hebrews concerning Abraham, but with more definiteness, here is One, not only as good as dead, but dead. Nevertheless, His thoughts, His teaching, He Himself, guide and govern those movements of the race that tend toward its perfection and its permanence. This is the supreme wonder, the wonder of all wonders.

When we turn to this last historic pamphlet of the New Testament and read the story of the new beginning of the Christian movement after the resurrection and ascension of our Lord, we find the secret of the victories that have resulted. In this second chapter of the Acts of the Apostles we have the account of the first blaze of light and the first thrill of power following the Resurrection and Ascension. The story is always full of fascination. We can never read this chapter without feeling the thrill of it and the power of it. The ideals suggested and revealed constitute the reason of this perpetual appeal rather than the realization of these things by the men of apostolic times, for the book of the Acts is as surely a revelation of failure as it is of victory. I do not know how far it is wise to take comfort from that fact, but I do find my own heart perpetually comforted by it. In these days of lamentation and wailing over the failure of the Christian church I go back to the beginning and find the same story still. Through all the centuries victories seem to have been in spite of unfaithfulness rather than as the result of faithfulness.

That which began at Pentecost is abiding. There is no need to pray for a new Pentecost. There can be no new Pentecost. Pentecost was the occasion when the Spirit of God came to create and abide with the church of God, and He has never been withdrawn. This place of our assembly is as full of the presence and power of that Holy Spirit of God as was the Upper Room at Jerusalem. We may not hear the sound of a rushing mighty wind, but the Spirit is proceeding from the Father through the Son into the lives of believing men and women and still is that selfsame Spirit poured upon all flesh.

Then it may be said, Where is the secret of present failure? How is it that we are not conscious of the same experience? In answer to that, two things must be said. First, there were experiences of the day of Pentecost that were not intended to abide. Things that were necessary at the moment have passed, but the spiritual facts have not passed. We do not ask for the sound of the rushing mighty wind, we do not seek—if we have spiritual apprehension of the true meaning of this Pentecostal effusion—for manifest tongues of fire upon the heads of the assembled saints. But, second, we do ask for the power itself, and we do most earnestly desire to know something of the experience that came to these people, that filled them with ecstasy, with joy; that irradiated their faces and put songs on lips which had perhaps never sung before. We do desire to know the secrets of that power which made prophecy prevailing in those olden days and constrained men to obedience to the Lord Christ. To know the power of this Pentecostal effusion surely we must discover its laws, and any measure of present failure is the result of failure in that particular.

The first symbol of the Christian church was the tongue of fire. The first experience of the outpoured Spirit was fullness of life and fullness of joy. This fullness of life and joy was expressed in that strange, I had almost said weird, manifestation in which men in various tongues praised God. The tongue was not a gift enabling men to preach or prophesy, it was a gift for praise. The first function of the Christian church is that of praise. The first function of the Christian priesthood is eucharistic in the true sense of that great word, that of the offering of thanksgiving and praise. When the Spirit of life fell on these men their eyes were opened, and they saw as they never had seen, and understood as they never had understood, things concerning Christ and concerning God. The multitudes listening heard them in their own tongues showing forth the mighty works of God. They had become a company of priests offering praise. In fullness of life there was fullness of joy, and out of that came the words which magnified the name of God and sounded His praise abroad.

The first impression this church produced on the city was that of mental arrest: they were compelled to consider; it was that of mental defeat: they were unable to explain; it was that of mental activity: they attempted to explain. The city was arrested, not by a preacher, but by a Spirit-filled church. That church, manifesting the fullness of its life in great joy, in great ecstasy, and in praise, created the opportunity for the Christian preacher to proclaim the evangel of Jesus.

The first activity in the power of the Spirit on behalf of men outside the company of the saints was that of this discourse of Peter. Observe the scheme of it. The people of the city said, "What meaneth *this?*" (Acts 2:12). Peter replied, "Be *this* known unto you, and give ear unto my words" (v. 14), and then proceeded to detailed explanation, of which the central declaration was, "*This* is that which hath been spoken by the prophet Joel" (v. 16).` The address culminated in the word of the text, "He hath poured forth *this*, which ye see and hear." The city said, "What meaneth this?" Peter replied, "Be *this* known unto you; . . . *This* is that; . . . He hath poured forth *this*" (italics mine).

Now let us confine our attention to the last word of the answer of Peter to the inquiry of the city. We shall dwell on the "he" and on the "this," speaking first of the relation of the Pentecostal baptism to Christ, and, second, of the meaning of the Pentecostal baptism for the world.

The Relation of the Pentecostal Baptism to Christ

The relation of the Pentecostal baptism to Christ is most clearly declared. Having quoted from the prophecy of Joel and having declared that the signs which they saw and the circumstances in the midst of which they found themselves were in fulfillment of that prophecy, Peter arrested the attention of his hearers anew as he said, "Ye men of Israel, hear these words" (v. 22). Then in an orderly sequence he told the story of Jesus. First, he named the Lord, Jesus of Nazareth. This was His most familiar name, the one by which He had been known, the one that had been used by the disciples in love and by other men in contempt. Second, he declared the witness of the miracles to the perfection of His nature as he spoke of Him as "a man approved of God among you" (v. 22 KJV). Not a man that God approved, but a man that God demonstrated "by mighty works and wonders and signs," not which He wrought, but "which God did by Him in the midst of you, even as ye yourselves know." The miracles and wonders were works of God wrought through the absolute perfection of Christ's humanity. Then, immediately, he came to the last fact of which these men had been conscious:

"Him"—and after a parenthesis, "being delivered up by the determinate counsel and foreknowledge of God," which the men who heard him certainly could not understand—"ye by the hand of lawless men did crucify and slay."

In these words so far the apostle had massed all that these men knew of Jesus, the manifest things— Jesus of Nazareth, a Man demonstrated among you by God in miracles and wonders and signs, a Man crucified. Beyond this these men who listened were unable to go of their own knowledge.

But the apostle had much more to say. He followed the mission of Jesus into spiritual heights that these men could not understand. He told them, if I may use the terms of time in relation to eternity, of the events that had followed the Cross, which for them had ended the career of Jesus, "whom God raised up"; and "being therefore by the right hand of God exalted, and having received of the Father the promise of the Holy Ghost, He hath poured forth this." He has given to these men this fullness of life which expresses itself in the praises that have arrested the city, amazed, and made it critical.

As we read the story there is evident throughout conflict between grace and sin: the Divine activity beneficent in its intention toward men and human activity in its intention hostile to God. As we watch the course of our Lord's ministry revealed in this wonderful paragraph we see Him as the center of perpetual conflict between sin on the one hand and the grace of God on the other.

Mark the movement of sin. Sin first expressed itself in blindness in the presence of the revelation of the life of Jesus: His words and His works witnessing to truth, Himself demonstrated by God by the wonders He wrought; men were blind, not seeing, not understanding. Blinding their own eyes, hardening their own hearts, they moved ever more persistently into the mental mood of definite hostility. Sin expressed itself finally in the Cross, as there it refused the Kingship of

78 / Classic Sermons on the Holy Spirit

the Christ. That Cross was man's answer to everything Christ had said, to His spiritual conceptions, to His severe and awful moral requirements, to His offer of pardon and of grace. The Cross of Jesus Christ is the very center and ultimate of human sin.

At that point in the history, sin had done its worst: it had crucified the Lord of glory and laid His body to rest in the tomb. Sinning man could do no more, he had become impotent, he had wreaked his vengeance on Jesus. One can hardly feel anything other than contempt for the rude superstition that watched the body of a dead man.

But now through all the movement observe the activity of grace. In the life of Jesus grace revealed God and the will of God concerning man. Through that life of Jesus God was calling man back to Himself. What of the Cross? Has sin there won a victory? Is that the ultimate word, is grace defeated, is the intention of God defeated? In the course of the declaration we find that which was a parenthesis so far as the men who listened were concerned, "being delivered up by the determinate counsel and foreknowledge of God." None knew the Cross like that until after Pentecost. None saw the Cross so until he looked back at it in the light of the Resurrection. But looking back through the Resurrection and in the light of the Spirit, Peter and the rest saw God acting in the Cross in determined love, mastering sin in a mystery that baffles us, in darkness that we never can enter, darkness that has at its center light unapproachable. In that hour and mystery of the Cross God is seen dealing with the sin that had expressed itself ultimately therein, and so dealing with it as to be victorious over it.

We now take the next step as suggested in the address of the apostle. The victory was won, the Lord was raised from the dead and exalted. Then followed the Ascension. As in all reverence we follow the Man of Nazareth into the light and glory of the heavenly place, the Spirit through Peter interprets the activity of that sacred hour in words that entirely transcend our explanation. The declaration that the Lord "received of the Father the promise of the Holy Ghost" (v. 33) can be understood only as we follow our Lord into the light of the heavenly place and realize that He passed in as the representative One. In that moment man returned to God, and God returned to man in Christ. By the mystery of the wounds He bore He asked, as He said He would, for the Spirit, that He might bestow it upon all trusting souls. Not by right of His sinless humanity did He claim the Spirit, but by the right of His passion. Not for Himself did He claim the Holy Spirit, for was not the whole history of His earthly career the history of fellowship with the Spirit? Born of the Spirit, baptized of the Spirit, in the power of the Spirit, He entered on His ministry. In the great mystery of the passion was it not also true that through the eternal Spirit He offered Himself to God? Now risen Man and ascended Lord, in the presence of God He received the Spirit as the representative of those whom He had left behind, representing them by the very wounds He bore, representing them by the passion through which He had passed. When the Father gave Him the Spirit, to use still this mystic figurative language, He gave the Spirit to Him as representing those for whom He had been wounded and bruised, whose place He had taken in the mystery of the Cross by which He had overcome sin. He represented humanity as humanity's Savior. Then we reach the final word, descriptive of the final movement, "He hath poured forth this."

Thus the Spirit on the day of Pentecost came to these people in answer to the prayer of Jesus, not in answer to their praying, not even in answer to their obedience, but entirely and absolutely in answer to the request in heavenly places of Christ Himself, the One whose wounds told the story of His conflict, and whose presence there proclaimed the fact of His victory. The Spirit thus given through the Son united those on whom He fell to the Son in a life of absolute identity, ultimately making those to whom He came like the Son.

If we have received the Spirit we have received it from the Father and through His Son. If we who name His name are receiving His Spirit, we are receiving the Spirit through the Son, not in answer to our praying, not as a reward for some sacrifice we are making. All these may be conditions that we fulfill, but this great Pentecostal gift of the Spirit, making men and women one with the Lord, indwelling them so that the very life of the Lord is dominant within them, expressing the power of the Lord through them, is in answer to the prayer of the Lord and the result of what He did.

The Meaning of the Pentecostal Baptism for the World

What, then, was the meaning and what the value of this Pentecostal baptism for the world? It was the creation of the Christian church of God. That is a phrase I used carefully, *the Christian church of God*. The church of God, if you will, but there had been a church of God in some senses before this. In the seventh chapter of this book of the Acts we have mentioned the church in the wilderness, that is the assembly, the congregation, the *ecclesia* in the wilderness. This, however, was the *Christian* church of God. It is an interesting fact that the phrase, the church of Christ, is used only once in the New Testament, and then by an apostle speaking of local churches. This church of God, the Christian church of God, is a new entity, a new nation, a new people. The differences between this church of God born at Pentecost and the church of God existing before are vital differences, but we need not now stay to look at them. In that moment, when those who had been individual disciples were brought into living union with the Lord Himself and so into living union with each other, the Christian church was born.

What, then, is the church in the world, considering it as a whole? It is God's institute of praise, God's institute of prayer, and God's institute of prophecy.

The whole church is, first of all, an institute created to praise God. "Ye are an elect race, a royal priesthood, a holy nation, a people for God's own possession, that ye may shew forth the excellencies of him who called you out of darkness into His marvellous light" (1 Peter 2:9). The first purpose of the church is that she shall praise God. I think we need to remember that in its first application, and its simplest, the first function of the Christian life is that of praising. Yet let us take the larger outlook. The Christian church exists so to reveal God as to utter forth His praise, so to make God known to men who know Him not that in the presence of the revelation they may be filled with awe and wonder, and amazement; so to make God known that God shall be attractive to humanity. Whether we are prepared to accept the declaration or not, the experience abides. Men of the world can know God only as God is revealed to them through His people. The Word of God can be powerful only as it is incarnate. Is not that the meaning of the central mystery of our holy religion? God came no nearer to humanity when Jesus was born in Bethlehem, but He came into visibility, into manifestation. In proportion as in this church of Jesus Christ His life is reproduced, God is being revealed anew. Our first business is that of praising Him, praising Him with lip and with life, in the actual songs we sing, in the hallelujahs we lift; praising Him by all the habits of our lives, by the perpetual testimony of our ways as they announce the fact of His being, the fact of His love. That was the first effect the church produced. Filled with life, light flashed from the eyes of the disciples, songs were on their lips, they magnified the mighty works of God, and the city was compelled to listen. In that hour of Pentecost God created for Himself by the coming of the Spirit through Christ a people for His own praise and glory, a kingdom of priests, that they might offer to Him sacrifices of praise and thanksgiving. Unless Pentecost produces in our lives fullness of joy and makes us a people filled with praise we are failing sadly. The first function of the Christian church is that she should be to the praise of God.

In that hour, moreover, *God created in the world a great institute of prayer*, for the function of the priesthood is not only eucharistic, it is intercessory. By the coming of the Spirit He created a people able to pray. Surely this is what the apostle meant in his Roman letter when he spoke of creation groaning and travailing in its pain, and then spoke of the church in the midst of the groaning creation, the church groaning and travailing together with creation in pain; and at last declared that "the Spirit himself maketh intercession for us with groanings that cannot be uttered" (Rom. 8:26). The Spirit of God understanding the pain of creation is grieved thereby, sorrow is caused in the very heart of God by the agony of humanity; that Spirit indwelling a company of people interprets to them the agony of creation, so that they enter into a new compassionate sympathy with all the suffering of the world, and thus in the midst of the groaning creation they constitute an institute of prayer. No man can pray for the world unless the Spirit interpret to him the world's agony, and the Spirit cannot interpret the world's agony to any man unless that man live in the midst of the world's agony. Not by retirement from the world, not by hiding away within a monastic institution, not by seeking to develop my own spiritual life by removing myself from the agony of the world can I ever pray for the world. But because I live every day in the midst of its busy life, am close to it and know it, and because the Spirit of God in me leads me into the secret of the deepest meaning of the world's agony and pain so that I no longer treat it as a superficial disease that can be dealt with by the nostrums of humanity, but as a great heart trouble that needs blood and sacrifice to deal with it, am I able to pray. Out of that revelation of the meaning of the world's agony created by the Spirit in the hearts of believing men, they are able to pray. The church of God in the economy of God was created an institute of prayer.

But more, *not for praise alone was the church created, not alone for prayer, but also for prophecy*, in the highest use of the great word, for proclamation. As with lip and life the saints praise, so by lip and life the saints should preach. The Spirit came uniting these men to the Lord, disannulling orphanage and canceling distance to make the risen and ascended Christ a living, bright reality. By so doing He enabled these men to speak to the Lord familiarly as those who have constant comradeship with Him, and by so doing enabled them to reveal the Lord of whom they spoke in tone and temper and habit and speech and in all activity. Reverently and superlatively, He came to multiply and unite in the perfect humanity of Nazareth all the scattered members of the one great Christ o'er all the earth that in the case of all of them, and not only in the case of the overseers, bishops, deacons, both by their preaching and their living they might show forth the glory of God and proclaim the power of His great evangel.

In conclusion, let us recognize that our possession of this power of Pentecost depends on our relation to Christ. Glancing at the description that Peter gave of the progress of our Lord toward the heights, we described it as a conflict between sin and grace. The question for our hearts is this, in such conflict, on which side are we? Are we in true fellowship with God in the determination of His grace to deal with sin in its opposition to the way and will of God, [or are we] refusing to come in obedience to the revelation of life, refusing to yield ourselves to the claims of the Christ? Such questions must be left unanswered in great assemblies. They are for answer only in the privacy of the individual life.

Perchance the question may be stated in another way. Let it thus be asked in individual lives. What is the influence we exert? The answer to that is the answer to the question whether or not we have this Spirit of Christ. "If any man hath not the Spirit of Christ, he is none of his" (Rom. 8:9). If any man be living still the life of blindness to all the will of God, the life of rebellion against the will of God, the life that in its practical activity refuses to crown Christ, that is demonstration of the fact that such a man lacks the Spirit of God. On the other hand, are we conscious that we have seen the glory, that in some measure at any rate already we have put the crown on the brow of Christ, and that the deepest passion of heart and life is to crown Him and make Him known to others? Then we may take heart and know by that sign that this Spirit of God has been given to us. As to whether we may be living in all the fullness and privilege of the Spirit is another question. The question that demands our earnest attention is, Are we ministers who praise His name in lip and life; do we know the secret of prayer that prevails in the midst of the world's agony; are we proclaiming the evangel in our words and in our works? If not, then let us search our hearts now and discover whether we have been self-deceived and lack the Spirit of God. As the Spirit comes we receive all that we need in order to praise and pray and prophesy. He comes in response to our belief in the living Lord at the commencement. He perpetually comes and proceeds, flowing in, filling and overflowing, in response to the attitude of belief maintained.

The celebration of a festival is of no profit save as we yield ourselves to all the facts that we celebrate. May it be ours, then, to know that union with the Lord in life and service that can come only by the presence and power of the Spirit.

NOTES

The Spirit's Work in Believers

Charles Simeon (1759–1836) was ordained in the Church of England in 1783 and ministered at the Church of the Holy Trinity, Cambridge, until his death. Under his leadership, the church became a vibrant center for evangelical preaching, evangelism, and world missions. He was one of the founders of the Church Missionary Society and greatly influenced Henry Martyn, missionary to India and Persia (Iran). Simeon said that he had three purposes in his ministry: to exalt Jesus Christ, to humble sinners, and to promote holy living.

This message is from *Let Wisdom Judge*, a collection of Simeon's university addresses edited by Arthur Pollard and published in 1959 by InterVarsity Press.

Charles Simeon

7

THE SPIRIT'S WORK IN BELIEVERS

> If any man have not the Spirit of Christ, he is none of his (Romans 8:9).

IN ENTERING ON THIS closing part of our subject, I feel peculiar difficulty, not from any want of scriptural and incontrovertible materials which, being wholly of an experimental nature, can only commend themselves to those who, by actual experience, are qualified to judge of them. There are, as we all know, different kinds of life—vegetable, animal, and rational—each rising above the other, and each, in its order, evincing a manifest superiority above that which is below it. But there is a fourth kind of life of which the Scripture speaks, namely, a spiritual life, which rises as far above the rest as any one of them does above another. All have their proper powers, which, however, they cannot exceed. The vegetable life has productiveness but no consciousness nor activity. The animal life has feeling but no perception of the deductions of reason. The rational life apprehends moral truth but forms no just conception of things that are spiritual. The spiritual life is exercised on things that are matters of pure revelation which reason is not of itself able to apprehend.

But I wish to guard against a common misapprehension respecting this spiritual life. It is by no means correct to speak of it as constituting a new *sense,* for then it would be a man's misfortune only, and not his fault, if he did not possess it. But it is correct to say that the spiritual man has a spiritual *perception*, which the natural man does not possess. The merely rational man has a film before his eyes; he views things through the medium of sense and not of faith, and the medium through which he looks at objects distorts them, if it does not altogether hide them from his sight. But in the spiritual man, the Holy Spirit, as "eyesalve," clears away the film and enables him to discern things as they really are. Faith also assists him by bringing remote objects with greater clearness to his mind. The power of the telescope to bring to our view things that are invisible to the naked eye is well known. Now this is the office and effect of faith, which enables us, if I may so speak, to behold both God Himself and the hidden mysteries of God, and to obtain a clear perception of things that are altogether beyond the reach of the eye of sense.

It appears, therefore, that the merely rational man labors under a twofold disadvantage in comparison with the spiritual man. He looks through a dense medium of sense that distorts, or altogether conceals, the objects before him, and he lacks that peculiar glass of faith that would present them truly and bring them, if I may so say, directly upon the retina of his mind. This is what Saint John means when he says, "the light shineth in darkness; and the darkness comprehended it not" (John 1:5), and this is, in very explicit terms, declared by Saint Paul to be a matter of universal experience. "The natural man [whoever he may be] receiveth not the things of the Spirit of God: for they are foolishness unto him [being seen by him only in a distorted view]: neither can he know them, because they are spiritually discerned [and he wants that spiritual perception, whereby alone he can truly apprehend them]. But he that is spiritual judgeth all things [having a clear and just perception of them], yet he himself is judged of no man [for it were a downright absurdity for a blind man to sit in judgment on one who sees]. For who [i.e., what merely natural man] hath known the mind of the Lord, that he may instruct him [the spiritual man]? But we [we who are spiritual] have the mind of Christ [and are, therefore, able to judge both ourselves and others]" (1 Cor. 2:14–16).

But while I speak thus in order to guard against misapprehension, I well know that there are many, very many, in the midst of us who can form the most accurate judgment of all we say, and who, if not in relation to every word, will yet as a whole set their seal to the truth of it. And, therefore, I hesitate not to lay before you what I verily believe to be in perfect accordance with God's revealed will, though on a subject so recondite and mysterious.

I am not, however, without a consciousness (and with deep grief I utter it) that under a profession of bringing forth only scriptural truth some have given vent to the veriest absurdities, talking about dreams and visions and arrogating to themselves I know not what claims of preternatural endowments. But against all such fancies and conceits I would enter my most solemn protest. The truth of God, though elevated above reason, is in perfect accordance with reason, and by *its reasonableness as a part of divine revelation* would I wish every word that I utter to be tried. I ask nothing more than this, that as God, of His own sovereign will and pleasure, bestows on some greater *natural* gifts than on others, so He may act in reference to *spiritual* gifts; and that as all our natural faculties are called forth into action by things *visible*, our hopes and fears, and joys and sorrows, being excited by them according to the interest we have in them, so our spiritual faculties may be called into action by things *invisible*, even by all the wonders of redeeming love, according as the blessings of redemption are manifested to the soul and our interest in them is made the one subject of our present and prospective happiness.

Having premised thus much, I now come to show *what the Holy Spirit will work in us when we are Christ's.* We must never forget that the Holy Spirit unites with the Lord Jesus Christ in the whole of His mediatorial office, though each sustains and executes in a more appropriate way that part which has been assigned Him by the Father. And if any of us be washed and justified and sanctified, it is in the name of the Lord

Jesus, and by the Spirit of our God (see Matt. 28:19). But it is the Spirit's office to which I must confine myself. While I address myself to this arduous and momentous subject, may the Lord Jesus Christ Himself be with us, as He has promised, and baptize us with the Holy Spirit and with fire, to consume the dross that is within us and to kindle in our hearts an inextinguishable flame of love toward His blessed name! The Holy Spirit, then, will perform in us the offices of *a Teacher, a Sanctifier, a Comforter*.

The Holy Spirit as a Teacher

Let us view Him first as a Teacher. The young convert knows little beyond the first principles of the oracles of God (Heb. 5:12). He is like a person just landed on a newly-discovered country, the beauty and riches of which he has yet to learn. But the Holy Spirit of Christ will open things to us gradually, as we are able to bear them, even as the Lord Jesus Himself did when on earth to His disciples. With increased knowledge, He will give us senses proportionably exercised to discern good and evil and thus will lead us on unto perfection (see Heb. 5:14–6:1).

The fundamental doctrine of salvation by faith is known by us when we first come to Christ, but there is much that as yet is very indistinctly seen. For instance, the nature and difficulty of the Christian warfare is yet but very partially discovered. The deceitfulness and desperate wickedness of the human heart is but little known (in fact, who but God can know it to its full extent?). The deceitfulness of sin also is by no means clearly discerned. As for the devices of Satan, the young believer is still ignorant of them to a great extent, and of the wiles whereby that subtle adversary deludes the souls of men he has scarcely any conception (Eph. 6:11; see 2 Cor. 2:11). Little does he imagine what power that old serpent has to beguile the minds of the simple and to corrupt them, even as he deceived our mother Eve, from the simplicity that is in Christ (2 Cor. 11:3; see Rom. 16:18).

Armor is provided for him against that great enemy of souls, but he knows not yet how to use it so as to defeat him who is but too justly called Apollyon. He has in his hand the Word of God, which is the sword of the Spirit," but he knows not how to use it with effect. He is unskillful in the word of righteousness. It is not until after many conflicts that he learns what are the parts on which he is most open to assault, what are the stratagems whereby that wily adversary most successfully ensnares him, and what are the means by which he is to ensure the victory over all his assailants. In the spiritual warfare, as in that which is temporal, experience can be gained only by active service. There is, however, this difference between them. In temporal warfare proficiency is the result of human ingenuity, whereas in the spiritual warfare it is the Spirit of God alone who can inspire us with the knowledge and address whereby we are to vanquish the legions of spirits that are combined against us (see Eph. 6:17–18).

But, further, the Holy Spirit will also discover to us the fullness and excellency of the Gospel salvation. As I have already acknowledged, the plan of salvation is understood by the veriest babe in Christ. But the excellency of it will be more and more developed to him, until, from the obscurity of the morning dawn, he attains the fuller light of the meridian sun. According as it is written by the prophet, "Then shall we know, if we follow on to know the LORD: his going forth is prepared as the morning" (Hos. 6:3), and as Solomon also has assured us, "The path of the just is as the shining light, that shineth more and more unto the perfect day" (Prov. 4:18). The young Christian knows little of that covenant to which all our salvation must ultimately be traced, the covenant entered into between the Father and the Son for the redemption of our fallen race. In this covenant, Christ, on the one part, undertook to stand in our place and stead and to endure, in His own Person, the penalty that we had incurred; the Father, on the other part, both gave to Him a chosen people, and engaged to accept them as righteous, on account of what He should do and suffer for them (John 17:2, 6, 9, 11–12, 24). This covenant is ordered in all things, and sure, and the blessings of it are all treasured up for us in Christ, our great Head and Representative, and are thus secured to us forever. As Paul writes to the Colossians, our life is hid with Christ in God; therefore, when Christ, who is our life, shall appear, we also shall appear with Him in glory (Col. 3:3–4). These blessings, too, are to be received from Him simply through the exercise of faith, that thus they "might be sure to all the seed" (Rom. 4:16), for no human being could ever have hoped to possess them if they had been committed to any other depository or if the attainment of them had been suspended on the strength and fidelity of man.

To unfold these things to the soul is the Holy Spirit's office. For this end He is given to us as an unction that shall abide with us and that shall, to a certain degree, by the clearness of His communications supersede the necessity for human instruction (1 John 2:27). And being given to us for this end, He enables the believer gradually to delve more and more deeply into this mystery, which the human eye cannot penetrate, at least not so as to behold its excellency (Eph. 1:17–18). These are among the deep things of God, which the Spirit alone searches, even the things which eye hath not seen, nor ear heard, neither have entered into the heart of man, but which are revealed to the soul by the Spirit of God and can be known in no other way (see 1 Cor. 2:9–12). True, these things are written plainly in the inspired volume, even as the figures are engraven with the utmost possible plainness on the sundial. But both in the one case and in the other are they written in vain until light is vouchsafed from heaven to shine upon them. Then only does the gnomon perform its office in the one, and then only is the end answered for the illumination of the soul in the other. Until that takes place, the natural man, how learned soever he be in other respects, will never discern aright the things of the Spirit of God. They will be no better than foolishness to him.

Thus taught of God, the believer has a knowledge of the Deity of which he had scarcely the slightest notion before. What astonishing views has he of the wisdom of God in devising such a plan whereby God's own justice might be duly satisfied and His mercy flow down to man in perfect consistency with all His other attributes! When he contemplates the goodness of God thus exercised, the holiness of God thus honored, the truth of God thus kept inviolate, and all the perfections of God thus harmonizing and glorified, and all this for *him*, he is perfectly astounded. He knows not how to believe it; it seems to him all as a mere parable (compare Ezek. 20:49). But seeing how suited all this is to his necessities and how sufficient for his wants and that in any other way than this he could find no more ground of hope for himself than for the fallen angels, he is *forced* to believe it. He sees that it is revealed in the Bible as with a sunbeam and established by evidence that admits not of the slightest doubt. And when he sees further that it has a transforming efficacy upon all who receive it, he is *constrained* to receive it as the very truth of God and to say, "Lord, to whom shall we go? thou hast the words of eternal life. And we believe and are sure that thou art that Christ, the Son of the living God" (John 6:68–69).

I give these things as samples only of what the Holy Spirit will effect in the believing soul as a Teacher. For the same powerful agency is extended to every part of divine truth and to every part, also, of Christian experience, seeing that He is expressly promised to guide us into all truth, that so, by His effectual teaching, we may know all things (see John 16:13; 1 John 2:20).

The Holy Spirit as a Sanctifier

But we will next consider His operations under the office of a Sanctifier. In this view we speak of Him in our catechism as "sanctifying the elect people of God." In fact, all that He does as a Teacher is in order to His work as a Sanctifier. Does He reveal Christ in us so as to give us brighter views of His Person and a more comprehensive knowledge of His work and offices? It is by this revelation that "we . . . beholding as in a glass the glory of the Lord, are changed into the same image from glory to glory, even as by the Spirit of the Lord" (2 Cor. 3:18). Does He further enable us to comprehend the breadth and length, and depth and height, and to know with progressive clearness and certainty the love of Christ which passes knowledge? It is so that we may be thereby filled with all the fullness of God (see Eph. 3:17–19).

With increasing knowledge He gives an increase of spiritual perception and with that perception, a spiritual appetite and with the appetite, a spiritual attainment. And this continues to advance until the soul with all its powers is brought into captivity to the obedience of Christ (2 Cor. 10:5). I think the whole process, though above the conception of the highest archangel, may be brought down, for all practical purposes, to the apprehension of a child. Our blessed Lord compares it to the wind, which is mighty in operation but visible only in its effects. It blows when and where it listeth, but we cannot tell either whence it comes, or whither it goes, yet of its agency we have no doubt whatever (John 3:8). The veriest child acknowledges it, while the wisest philosopher is unable adequately to explain it.

The magnet would furnish us with a similar illustration of this truth, for its influence, if not rendered visible by actual experience, would not be credited. But there is another natural process that will give us a fuller, and, perhaps I may say, a more distinct, apprehension of this mysterious subject. A river flowing from its source in one current to the ocean may serve to show us the natural man, with all his faculties both of body and mind, departing from God and proceeding with fatal indifference and perseverance until he is finally lost in that abyss from which there is no return. But within a certain distance from the sea we may behold that same river arrested in its course by the tide and returning with equal rapidity toward its fountainhead. And in that we may behold the sinner returning to his God. Even from the partial back currents that are occasioned by local obstacles we may behold the parallel yet more strikingly illustrated. For in either case these may serve to show that as in man's departure from God there are some risings of compunction and some little, though ineffectual, restraints from the remonstrances of an accusing conscience, so in the believer's return to God there are some remnants of corruption which betray a want of that completeness of soul which he will enjoy in a better world.

But the point particularly to be noticed is this. How is this change effected? How is it effected in the river? Is it through the power and instrumentality of man? No; it is by the invisible, but powerful, attraction of the moon. The operation of the moon is not seen but in its effects, yet it is not on that account denied. The effects are unquestionable, nor can they reasonably be traced to any other cause. At all events they cannot in the smallest possible degree be ascribed to man. And how is the change effected upon the souls of men? It is the Holy Spirit who operates upon them to bring them back to God. True, His operations are not seen except in the effects produced by them. But those effects infinitely exceed all human power, and in the unerring Word of God they are ascribed to the Holy Spirit whose peculiar office it is not only to regenerate us at first, but progressively to form us after the divine image and to render us meet for our heavenly inheritance (see Titus 3:3–5).

That there are defects in the best of men is certain, but that only makes the analogy more complete. There are and will be intervening obstacles that will, at some times and under peculiar circumstances, interfere with the believer's progress. But these do not interrupt his general course or give any just cause for questioning the influence under which he moves. His habitual walk is not after the flesh, but after the Spirit (see Rom. 7:18–24; 8:1, 5). We have said that the work is progressive. He goes from grace to grace, from victory to victory, growing up into Christ in all things, until he arrives at the measure of the stature of the fullness of Christ (Eph. 4:13; compare 2 Peter 3:18). At first he is represented in the Scriptures as a child, then as a young man, and then as a father (see 1 John 2:12–14); the work in his soul is compared to the corn, which appears first in the blade, then the ear, after that the full corn in the ear (Mark 4:28). These very comparisons show that the believer is not at first all that he will be at a future period. His heart will be more and more weaned from earthly things and be fixed with more and more intensity on things above, until he is altogether changed into the image of his God in righteousness and true holiness (Eph. 4:24).

This advance toward maturity will be more or less visible to all around him. There will be in him more solidity, more uniformity, more consistency. His principles will be more and more commended to all around him by their efficacy to beautify his soul and to adorn his life (see 1 Peter 3:3–4). In a word, he will be renewed, not in his mind only, but in the spirit of his mind (see Eph. 4:23) and will become an epistle of Christ known and read of all men, an epistle not written by any human hand, but by the Spirit of the living God (2 Cor. 3:2–3). He will be in himself (and will constrain all who know him to acknowledge that he is) what the Scriptures emphatically call a *man of God* (2 Tim. 3:17).

The Holy Spirit as a Comforter

And what is the result of all this? It is that in and by the whole of this work the Holy Spirit performs the office of a Comforter. Under this character, the world knows Him not, neither can receive Him. But believers do know Him, for He dwells with them and shall be in them throughout the whole of their earthly pilgrimage (John 14:16–17). Even at their first coming to Christ, the Holy Spirit in some measure discharges this office, speaking peace to their troubled consciences and enabling them to rejoice in their unseen but beloved Savior (1 Peter 1:8). This was eminently conspicuous on the day of Pentecost when the whole multitude of believers, who had just before been filled with terror, ate their meat with gladness and singleness of heart, praising God (Acts 2:46–47). But through the whole course of their future lives He carries on this work, revealing Christ more and more clearly to them and applying the promises with sweet assurance to their souls. Hence the word so applied is said to work "by the power of the Spirit of God," and to come to men, "not . . . in word only, but also in power, and in the Holy Ghost, and in much assurance." And the Holy Spirit Himself is called the "holy Spirit of promise," because in this way He makes use of the promises for their good (see Rom. 15:19; 1 Thess. 1:5; Eph. 1:13).

Thus He performs the office of a Comforter toward Christ's redeemed people. He gives them near access to God in prayer. In their supplications He helps their infirmities and makes intercession for them, and in them, "according to the will of God" (Rom. 8:26–27; see Eph. 2:18; Jude 20). He is in them a Spirit of adoption, enabling them to go to God with confidence, crying, "Abba, Father"; shedding abroad God's love in their hearts, He witnesses with their spirits that they are children of God (Rom. 8:15–16). In this way, also, He establishes them in Christ and seals them unto the day of redemption and is within them an earnest of their heavenly inheritance (see 2 Cor. 1:21–22; Eph. 1:14). An "earnest" is a part of a payment, and a pledge of the remainder. Such is the Holy Spirit in the believer's soul, giving him to possess already a measure of the heavenly felicity and assuring to him, in due season, the full and everlasting possession of it. In a season of affliction especially do the communications of His grace abound. We read of those who "received the word in much affliction, with joy of the Holy Ghost" (1 Thess. 1:6), and in proportion as any person's afflictions abound, the Holy Spirit will make His consolations to abound with still greater and more transcendent efficacy (2 Cor. 1:5).

It is worthy, however, of observation that the comforts that He administers at an earlier and at a more advanced period are, for the most part, widely different. The one is rather of a tumultuous nature, the other more serene; the one more transient, the other more abiding. The one elevates the spirits of a man on account of the good that has accrued to him; the other humbles and abases his soul on account of his great unworthiness. The one is a fire recently kindled in which there is a considerable mixture of flame and smoke; the other is like a fire that has become bright and solid and burns with an unobtrusive but mighty efficacy. In confirmation of what I have said I need only add that this is the very description that God Himself has given us of His kingdom. It consists, we are told, not in externals of any kind, but in "righteousness, and peace, and joy in the Holy Ghost" (Rom. 14:17).

And now, will anyone say that these blessings were peculiar to the apostolic age and are not to be expected by us? What then is the meaning of that interrogation which Saint Paul addressed to the whole Corinthian church, "Know ye not that ye are the temple of God, and that the Spirit of God dwelleth in you?" And, again, "Know ye not your own selves, how that Jesus Christ is in you, except ye be reprobates?" (1 Cor. 3:16; 2 Cor. 13:5). Hence it is evident that this is a truth of which we must not only have the actual experience, but a consciousness also that it is realized in us. And the man who questions it as a matter of Christian experience has yet to learn the very first principles of the Christian faith. For even to the murderers of our Lord did Saint Peter on the day of Pentecost announce that this blessing should be theirs, and that too even to their latest posterity: "Repent, and be baptized every one of you in the name of Jesus Christ for the remission of sins, and ye shall receive the gift of the Holy Ghost. For the promise is unto you, and to your children, and to all that are afar off, even as many as the Lord our God shall call" (Acts 2:38–39). In fact, this is the promise that was originally made to Abraham for himself and all his believing posterity, whether of the Jewish or Gentile world, even "the promise of the Spirit through faith" (Gal. 3:14).

This objection being set aside, therefore, I confidently ask whether I have carried any one of these matters to excess, either requiring more than the Scriptures require, or promising more than the Scriptures promise? I can truly say that I have exercised all possible caution on this head. I know and lament that there are crude and enthusiastic conceits entertained by some who would have us believe that they are actuated by certain divine impulses irrespective of the Word as the medium of conveying them and in despite of the vanity and folly which they themselves betray as their invariable result. But I trust that not one word that I have spoken can be thought to have countenanced any such conceits as these. The written Word is the medium by which the Spirit works and the standard by which His agency must be tried. And if His operations do not produce holiness, as well as light and comfort, they are no better than a delusion, a desperate and a fatal delusion. The offices of the Holy Spirit cannot be separated from each other. He is a Teacher, a Sanctifier, and a Comforter.

I advisedly place the office of a Sanctifier between the other two because it is equally connected both with that which precedes and with that which follows. It is connected with that which precedes as the end for which divine teaching is administered, and with that which follows as that without which no true comfort can possibly exist. I entreat, then, that you will all look for the gift of the Holy Spirit to impart to you these blessings. And I declare before God that no one of you will ever behold the face of God in peace if you do not both desire and obtain the Holy Spirit for these ends. The word of God is immutable: "If any man have not the Spirit of Christ, he is none of his" (Rom. 8:9).

If any be disposed to deride the sacred influences of the Spirit, imputing to Satan, as it were, what is wrought by the Holy Spirit, let them beware of the sin against the Holy Spirit; they tread close upon it, if they do not actually commit it. I would have them remember that, in proportion to the light against which they offend and the malignity with which they utter their scoffs, they approach this fatal sin. And if once they do commit it, our blessed Lord declares that they shall never have forgiveness, either in this world, or in the world to come, and that they are therefore in danger of eternal damnation (see Matt. 12:32; Mark 3:28–29).

On the other hand, if any have experienced the workings of the Holy Spirit to bring them to Christ, let them watch and pray against temptation and sin of every kind lest, by any open or secret declension from the ways of God, they grieve and vex his holy Spirit, and quench His sacred motions, and thus the latter end is worse with them than the beginning (2 Peter 2:20; see Eph. 4:30; Isa. 63:10; 1 Thess. 5:19).

But I hope better things of this assembly, though I thus speak. Scoffers do not abound at this day as once they did. The truths of the Gospel are better understood, its mysteries are more justly appreciated, and, provided only that the deep things of God be stated with modesty and sobriety, they find a favorable acceptance now where once, perhaps, they would only have provoked a smile. On that head, therefore, I feel no occasion to dwell. But this very circumstance which renders a profession of piety more easy makes the danger of departing from it more imminent, since, as in the case of the stony-ground hearers in our Lord's parable, that which is hastily received is but too often as hastily relinquished. To every one of you then I say, "Hold that fast which thou hast, that no man take thy crown" (Rev. 3:11); or rather, look to the Lord Jesus Christ for more enlarged supplies of His Spirit, for He has received this gift for men, even for the most rebellious (see Ps. 68:18). Just as God has not given "the Spirit by measure unto him," so is there no measure fixed for the dispensation of the Spirit to us. It is our privilege not only to *have* the Spirit, but to be filled with the Spirit (see John 3:34; Eph. 5:18). Many of you, I would hope, have already received the firstfruits of the Spirit (Rom. 8:3), but be not satisfied with these. Christ came not only that you might have life but that you might have it more abundantly. He has promised to pour floods upon those who are thirsty (see John 10:10; Isa. 44:3). Yes, He would have you to live in the Spirit and walk in the Spirit and purify your souls by the Spirit and abound in hope through the Spirit and to be filled with joy in the Holy Spirit (see Gal. 5:25; 1 Peter 1:22; Rom. 15:13; Acts 13:52).

See to it, then, that you avail yourselves of these immense advantages and beg of God to pour out His Spirit more and more abundantly upon you through Jesus Christ that, being led in all things by the Spirit, ye may be, and give decisive evidence that ye are, the children of God. And may the Holy Spirit be so richly poured out upon us from on high that, as Isaiah foretold, this wilderness may become a fruitful field and the fruitful field be so luxuriant as to be counted for a forest! (Isa. 32:15).

On Grieving the Holy Spirit

John Wesley (1703–1781), with his brother Charles and with George Whitefield, founded the Methodist movement in Britain and America. On May 24, 1738, he had his great spiritual experience in a meeting at Aldersgate Street, when his "heart was strangely warmed" and he received assurance of salvation. Encouraged by Whitefield to do open-air preaching, Wesley soon was addressing thousands in spite of the fact that many churches were closed to him. The Methodist societies he formed became local churches that conserved the results of his evangelism. He wrote many books and preached over 40,000 sermons during his long ministry.

This sermon is taken from *Works of John Wesley*, volume 7, published by Zondervan Publishing House.

John Wesley

8

ON GRIEVING THE HOLY SPIRIT

> Grieve not the holy Spirit of God, whereby ye are sealed unto the day of redemption (Ephesians 4:30).

THERE CAN BE NO point of greater importance to him who knows that it is the Holy Spirit that leads us into all truth and into all holiness than to consider with what temper of soul we are to entertain His divine presence so as not either to drive Him from us or to disappoint Him of the gracious ends for which His abode with us is designed, which is not the amusement of our understanding, but the conversion and entire sanctification of our hearts and lives.

These words of the apostle contain a most serious and affectionate exhortation to this purpose. "Grieve not the holy Spirit of God, whereby ye are sealed unto the day of redemption."

The title "holy," applied to the Spirit of God, does not only denote that He is holy in His own nature but that He makes us so. He is the great fountain of holiness to His church, the Spirit from whence flows all the grace and virtue by which the stains of guilt are cleansed and we are renewed in all holy dispositions and again bear the image of our Creator. Great reason, therefore, there was for the apostle to give this solemn charge concerning it, and the highest obligation lies upon us all to consider it with the deepest attention. That we may the more effectually do, I shall inquire: First, in what sense the Spirit of God is said to be grieved at the sins of men; second, by what kind of sin He is more especially grieved; and third, I shall endeavor to show the force of the apostle's argument against grieving the Holy Spirit—by whom we are sealed to the day of redemption.

In What Sense Is the Spirit of God Grieved?

In what sense may the Spirit of God be said to be grieved with the sins of men? There is not anything of what we properly call passion in God. But there is something of an infinitely higher kind: some motions of His will, which are more strong and vigorous than can be conceived by men, although they have not the nature of human passions, yet will answer the ends of them. By grief, therefore, we are to understand a disposition in God's will, flowing at once from His boundless love to the persons of men and His infinite abhorrence of their sins. And in this restrained sense it is here applied to the Spirit of God in the words of the apostle.

And the reasons for which it is peculiarly applied to Him are, first, because He is more immediately present with us; second, because our sins are so many contempts of this highest expression of His love and disappoint the Holy Spirit in His last remedy; and, third, because, by this ungrateful dealing, we provoke Him to withdraw from us.

We are said to grieve the Holy Spirit by our sins because of His immediate presence with us. They are more directly committed under His eye, and are, therefore, more highly offensive to Him. He is pleased to look upon professing Christians as more peculiarly separated to His honor. We are so closely united to Him that we are said to be one spirit with Him, and, therefore, every sin that we now commit, besides its own proper guilt, carries in it a fresh and infinitely high provocation. "Know ye not," says Paul, "that your body is the temple of the Holy Ghost?" (1 Cor. 6:19). And how are our bodies so, but by His inhabitation and intimate presence with our souls? When, therefore, we set up the idols of earthly inclinations in our hearts (which are properly His altar), and bow down ourselves to serve those vicious passions that we ought to sacrifice to His will—this must needs be, in the highest degree, offensive and grievous to Him. For what concord is there between the Holy Spirit and Belial? or what agreement has the temple of God with idols? (see 2 Cor. 6:15–16).

We grieve the Holy Spirit by our sins because they are so many contempts of the highest expression of His love and disappoint Him in His last remedy whereby He is pleased to endeavor our recovery. And thus every sin we now commit is done in despite of all His powerful assistances, in defiance of His reproofs—an ungrateful return for infinite lovingkindness!

As the Holy Spirit is the immediate minister of God's will upon earth and transacts all the great affairs of the church of Christ—if while He pours out the riches of His grace upon us, He finds them all unsuccessful, no wonder if He appeals to all the world, in the words of the prophet, against our ingratitude: "And now, O . . . men of Judah, judge . . . betwixt me and my vineyard. What could have been done more to my vineyard, that I have not done in it? wherefore, when I looked that it should bring forth grapes, brought it forth wild grapes?" (Isa. 5:3–4). These, and many more such, which we meet with in the Holy Scriptures, are the highest expressions of the deepest concern such as imply the utmost unwillingness to deal severely even with those whom yet, by all the wise methods of His grace, He could not reform. The Holy Spirit here represents Himself as one who would be glad to spare sinners if He could, and therefore we may be sure it is grievous to Him that by their sins they will not suffer Him.

For men thus to disappoint the Holy Spirit of Love—for that too is His peculiar title—to make Him thus wait that He may be gracious, and pay attendance on us through our whole course of folly and vanity, and stand by and be a witness of our stubbornness, with the importunate offers of infinite kindness in His hands—is a practice of such a nature that no gracious mind can bear the thoughts of it. It is an argument of God's unbounded mercy, which He is pleased to express, that He is only grieved at it, that His indignation does not flame out against those who are thus basely ungrateful and consume them in a moment.

It was such ingratitude as this in the Jews, after numberless experiences of His extraordinary mercies toward them, that made infinite love, at last, turn in bitterness to reward them according to their doings, as we find the account given by the Prophets, in the most affecting and lively manner. And surely, considering the much greater obligations He has laid on us who enjoy the highest privileges, we may be sure that [the reward of] our sinful and untoward behavior will, at last, be as great as the mercies we have abused.

There is no doubt but God observes all the sons of men, and His wrath abides on every worker of iniquity. But it is the unfaithful professor who has known His pardoning love that grieves His Holy Spirit, which implies a peculiar baseness in our sins. A man may be provoked, indeed, by the wrongs of his enemy, but he is properly grieved by the offenses of his friend. And, therefore, besides our other obligations, our very near relation to God, as being His friends and children, would, if we had a spark of gratitude in our souls, be a powerful restraint upon us in preserving us from evil.

But if arguments of this kind are not strong enough to keep us from grieving our best Friend, the Holy Spirit of God, let us consider, that, *by this ungrateful conduct, we shall provoke Him to withdraw from us.*

The truth of this almost all who have ever tasted of the good gifts of the Holy Spirit must have experienced. It is to be hoped that we have had, some time or other, so lively a sense of His holy influence upon us that when we have been so unhappy as to offend Him, we could easily perceive the change in our souls, in that darkness, distress, and despondency which more especially follow the commission of willful and presumptuous sins. At those seasons, the blessed Spirit retired and concealed His presence from us, we were justly left to a sense of our own wretchedness and misery, until we humbled ourselves before the Lord and by deep repentance and active faith obtained a return of divine mercy and peace.

And the more frequently we offend Him, the more

we weaken His influences in our souls. For frequent breaches will necessarily occasion estrangement between us; it is impossible that our intercourse with Him can be cordial when it is disturbed by repeated interruptions. So a man will forgive his friend a great many imprudences and some willful transgressions, but to find him frequently affronting him, all his kindness will wear off by degrees. The warmth of his affection, even toward him who had the greatest share of it, will die away, as he cannot but think that such a one does not any longer either desire or deserve to maintain a friendship with him.

By What Kinds of Sin Is the Holy Spirit Grieved?

By what kinds of sin is the Holy Spirit especially grieved? These sins are, in general, such as either at first wholly disappoint His grace of its due effect upon our souls or are afterward directly contrary to His gracious and merciful assistances. Of the former sort, I shall only mention, at present, inconsiderateness; of the latter, sins of presumption.

The first I shall mention, as being more especially grievous to the Holy Spirit, is inconsiderateness and inadvertence to His holy motions within us. There is a particular frame and temper of soul, a sobriety of mind, without which the Spirit of God will not concur in the purifying of our hearts. It is in our power, through His preventing and assisting grace, to prepare this in ourselves, and He expects we should, this being the foundation of all His after-works. Now, this consists in preserving our minds in a cool and serious disposition, in regulating and calming our affections, and calling in and checking the inordinate pursuits of our passions after the vanities and pleasures of this world. The doing of this is of such importance that the very reason why men profit so little under the most powerful means is that they do not look enough within themselves—they do not observe and watch the discords and imperfections of their own spirits, nor attend with care to the directions and remedies that the Holy Spirit is always ready to suggest. Men are generally lost in the hurry of life, in the business or pleasures of it, and seem to think that their regeneration, their new nature, will spring and grow up within them with as little care and thought of their own as their bodies were conceived and have attained their full strength and stature. Whereas, there is nothing more certain than that the Holy Spirit will not purify our natures unless we carefully attend to His motions, which are lost upon us while, in the prophet's language, we "scatter away our time"—while we squander away our thoughts upon unnecessary things and leave our spiritual improvement, the one thing needful, quite unthought of and neglected.

There are many persons who, in the main of their lives, are regular in their conversation and observe the means of improvement and attend upon the holy sacrament with exactness, who yet, in the intervals of their duties, give too great liberty to their thoughts, affections, and discourse. They seem to adjourn the great business of salvation to the next hour of devotion. If these professors lose so much in their spiritual estate for want of adjusting and balancing their accounts, what then must we think of those who scarce ever bestow a serious thought upon their eternal welfare? Surely there is not any temper of mind less a friend to the spirit of religion than a thoughtless and inconsiderate one that, by a natural succession of strong and vain affections, shuts out everything useful from their souls, until, at length, they are overtaken by a fatal lethargy. They lose sight of all danger and become insensible of divine convictions, and, in consequence, quite disappoint all the blessed means of restoration. If, therefore, we measure the Holy Spirit's concern at the sins of men by the degrees of His disappointment, we may conclude that there is no state of mind that grieves Him more, unless that of actual wickedness.

Presumptuous sins are, indeed, in the highest manner offensive to the Holy Spirit of God. They are instances of open enmity against Him and have all the guilt of open rebellion. The willful sinner is not ignorant or surprised, but knowingly fights against God's express commandment and the lively, full, and present conviction of his own mind and conscience, so that this is the very standard of iniquity. And all other kinds of sins are more or less heinous, as they are nearer or farther off from sins of this dreadful nature, inasmuch as these imply the greatest opposition to God's will, contempt of His mercy, and defiance of His justice. This, if anything can, doubtless must so grieve Him as to make Him wholly withdraw His gracious presence.

The Force of the Apostle's Argument Against Grieving the Holy Spirit

I come now to show the force of the apostle's argument against grieving the Holy Spirit: Because we "are sealed unto the day of redemption."

By "the day of redemption" may be meant either the time of our leaving these bodies at death or of our taking them again at the general resurrection, though here it probably means the latter, in which sense the apostle uses the word in another place: "Waiting for the adoption, to wit, the redemption of our bodies" (Rom. 8:23). And to this day of redemption we are sealed by the Holy Spirit these three ways:

1. by receiving His real stamp upon our souls, being made the partakers of the divine nature;
2. by receiving Him as a mark of God's property, as a sign that we belong to Christ;
3. as an earnest and assurance to our own spirits that we have a title to eternal happiness.

First, *we are sealed by the Holy Spirit of God by our receiving His real stamp upon our souls,* being made the partakers of the divine nature and "meet for the inheritance of the saints in light." This is, indeed, the design of His dwelling in us: to heal our disordered souls and to restore that image of His upon our nature, which is so defaced by our original and actual corruptions. And until our spirits are, in some measure, thus renewed, we can have no communion with Him.

For "if we say that we have fellowship with him, and walk in darkness, we lie, and do not the truth" (1 John 1:6). But by the renewal of our minds in the image of Him that created us, we are still more capable of His influences. By means of a daily intercourse with Him, we are more and more transformed into His likeness, until we are satisfied with it.

This likeness to God, this conformity of our will and affections to His will, is, properly speaking, holiness; to produce this in us is the proper end and design of all the influences of the Holy Spirit. By means of His presence with us, we receive from Him a great fullness of holy virtues; we take such features of resemblance in our spirits as correspond to His original perfections. And thus we are sealed by Him, in the first sense, by way of preparation for our day of redemption.

And since we are so, and our new natures thus grow up under the same power of His hands, what do we, when we grieve Him by our sins, but undo and destroy His work? We frustrate His designs by breaking down the fences that He had been trying to raise against the overflowings of corruption, so that, at last, we entirely defeat all His gracious measures for our salvation.

We are sealed by the Holy Spirit to the day of redemption as a sign of God's property in us and as a mark that we belong to Christ. And this is, by His appointment, the condition and security of that future happiness, into which He will admit none but those who have received the Spirit of His Son into their hearts. But in whomsoever He finds this mark and character, when He shall come to judge the world, these will He take to Himself and will not suffer the destroyer to hurt them. To this very purpose the prophet Malachi, speaking of those who feared God, says, "They shall be mine, saith the LORD, . . . in that day when I make up my jewels" (Mal. 3:17)—that is to say, when I set my seal and mark upon them—"and I will spare them, as a man spareth his own son that serveth him."

Now, if the Holy Spirit be the sign, the seal, and the

security of our salvation, then, by grieving Him by our sins, we break up this seal with our own hands, we cancel our firmest security, and, as much as in us lies, reverse our own title to eternal life.

Besides this, *the Holy Spirit within us is the security of our salvation; He is likewise an earnest of it, and assures our spirits that we have a title to eternal happiness.* "The Spirit itself beareth witness with our spirit, that we are the children of God" (Rom. 8:16). And in order that this inward testimony may be lively and permanent, it is absolutely necessary to attend carefully to the secret operation of the Holy Spirit within us, who, by infusing His holy consolations into our souls, by enlivening our drooping spirits, and by giving us a quick relish of His promises, raises bright and joyous sensations in us and gives a man, beforehand, a taste of the bliss to which he is going. In this sense God is said, by the apostle to the Corinthians, to have "sealed us, and given the earnest of the Spirit in our hearts," and that earnest, not only by way of confirmation of our title to happiness, but as an actual part of that reward at present, the fullness of which we expect hereafter.

What God the Spirit Can Do for Us

Howard Frederick Sugden (1907–1993) was a gifted expositor and loving pastor with a winsome sense of humor and the ability to make the Scriptures come alive to the contemporary mind. During more than sixty years of service, he preached in conferences and churches in many parts of the world. He pastored three churches in Michigan, finishing his course as pastor of South Baptist church, Lansing, where he served for thirty-five years. He also pastored Central Baptist church, London, Ontario, Canada, for three years. A lover of good books, he built a large library and unselfishly shared his knowledge and wisdom with all who called upon him. He was "a pastor's pastor."

This message was delivered at the Moody Bible Institute Founder's Week conference in Chicago, on February 4, 1970, and is used by permission of the Moody Bible Institute.

Howard Frederick Sugden

9

WHAT GOD THE SPIRIT CAN DO FOR US

DAVID LAWRENCE, EDITOR OF *U. S. News and World Report*, made the observation the last month of the old year that there is a sense of impending disaster which pervades the whole world. I wish I had time this morning to read what newspapermen have said concerning the hour in which we live, men who are not Christians but men who look out upon the scene of today's world with great anxiety because they fear the disaster that threatens us.

It is a strange thing that we see happening in our society, because that which is in the world has a way of sneaking in the church of Jesus Christ. I am shocked when I hear men say that the era of Christendom is over. Others say people are in rebellion against the church. In fact, most religious leaders outside the church declare that the organizational structure of the church is over.

Now our Lord, standing upon the Mount of Olives, looked out upon the world, and then He looked at the disciples. He also looked across the centuries and anticipated every hour that would ever arise. I'm quite confident that He was aware of the failures. He was aware of those disciples and their weaknesses, yet He promised to give to them a power that would be greater than any power they would ever face. Luke is very careful in his writings to speak about this power. In the last chapter of Luke he records the Lord's promise to the disciples, Ye shall "be endued with power from on high" (Luke 24:49). When we come to Acts 1:5 we read: "John truly baptized with water; but ye shall be baptized with the Holy Ghost not many days hence," and verse 8, "But ye shall receive power, the Holy Spirit coming upon you" (author's translation).

Some of you are aware of Kittel's great work on Greek terminology. I was amazed to find that he gives thirty pages to the word *power*. Think of it—thirty pages on the word *power* and what it can mean in the context of human life. It's tough to read thirty pages, but it's something to discover that the word means that God can make us able. Regardless of how dark the day, how dismal it may be, how low the clouds, how deep the hours of our frustration, God moves in our lives to make us able. The word, Kittel says, can mean to make us capable. Think of God reaching down and taking fishermen, think of God reaching down and calling us, think of God stooping and catching us up and saying, "I'm going to take this man with all of his fears and failures and feebleness and I'm going to make him capable." The word also sometimes means capacity. I suppose when you take all this together, you see that God has given to us a capacity for Himself, a capacity that He alone can fill.

Luke affirmed to these disciples that there would be an hour of divine empowerment. The Holy Spirit who had moved upon Gideon and moved upon David and moved upon Isaiah and had moved upon other men of the Old Testament, this Holy Spirit was going to take up His abode and was going to indwell believers. We live so far this side of Pentecost that we forget the wonder of this. But imagine Peter nudging John and saying, "Think of that! Think of that! The same power that came into the life of Gideon, the same power that came into the lives of men in the Old Testament, this power is going to come to take up residence in us, to live in us. Man!"

And then the hour came on that unusual day, that day in history that was a day on God's calendar like Calvary, a day when God came into the world in a new way in the Holy Spirit. He had been in the world before, He had worked in men before. Now He came into the world in a new way. He came on the Day of Pentecost, and He baptized these individual believers into the body of Christ. They were not only baptized into the body of Christ, but they were filled. The book of Acts is the record of these men who moved out against the darkness of a pagan world, empowered by the Holy Spirit of God.

Sometimes when I talk with my brethren, we talk about the apostasy, we talk about the darkness, we talk about the hour in which we live. Then suddenly there comes the overwhelming sense that God is the same, that Jesus Christ is the same, that the Holy Spirit of God is the same, and the same power is available to us today as it was for those men in those days. Oh, I need to know the wonder of being filled with the Holy Spirit of God!

I discover that whenever the Holy Spirit is spoken of in the book of Acts and the terminology relates to the filling of the Spirit, that this power is always linked with virtue. The believers never had power in the book of Acts for the sake of power.

Now Lansing makes Oldsmobiles. They are the best car in the world. The reason I know is because they say so, and that ought to make it so, don't you think? I have a little F85 that has four on the ground, six on the floor, 300 under the hood, and I stand by and say, "I have a little car. It has this power," and it doesn't impress anybody. But when I get out on the expressways and I catch up to a truck that's sort of moping along, and I push down like that, it goes wheeeeee! Suddenly that power becomes relevant to the car in which it rests, and I go out on the highways to prove the point of power.

The Holy Spirit Gives Power to Witness

Notice in Acts 1:8: "But ye shall receive power, the Holy Spirit coming upon you, and ye shall be witnesses unto me." The Holy Spirit coming upon these early believers was going to work in their lives, and they were to be witnesses. The word has two meanings. The old Anglo-Saxon word for *witness* means to know. A witness gives what he knows. When these early believers went out, they simply said, "We cannot help speaking the things that we have experienced, that we have seen and we have heard." That's the Anglo-Saxon word for witness. There is another meaning, however; it is the word from which we get our word *martyr*. A witness then is an individual who knows something and is willing to die for it.

The Lord is very careful about the witness that we give. He said, "Ye shall be witnesses unto me." So we bear witness of the person of Jesus Christ and what He has wrought in our lives personally—a living Person beyond the reach of death who has met our needs, and we witness of Him. But in Luke 24:48 we are told, "Ye are witnesses of these things." When we go out to be a witness, we not only witness about the person of Jesus Christ, but also bear witness of these things recorded in Luke 24, a most magnificent record of the resurrection and the attendant miracles of that resurrection. It thrills my soul and gives me goose bumps when I think that there's a Man who died, who rose, who lives, and I am to be a witness of that resurrection and these things.

What were the things of which they were to bear witness? They were to bear witness of how He entered into the common experiences of life. Talk about relevancy! He walked with them along the road. Here is our Lord walking with two people, an old man and his wife, Mr. and Mrs. Cleopas along that road. He not only walked with them, He stopped in their little cottage.

As they got near Emmaus, she nudged her husband and said, "Ask Him to stop for tea." And He stopped, and when He came in He came in not as a guest but as a host. He just took over. I am to go out to tell how this Christ relates to my life in every area of life, and I tell you, there is a waiting world outside that needs to know the wonder of this risen, living Christ and how He relates to them, not as sort of an ethereal tapioca pudding sort of something, but He comes to us in power. I'm to be a witness.

I've always been interested in law. I've never been involved with the law, but I'm interested in it. So whenever I had a chance, I would spend a little time in court watching judges and lawyers. The other day I was subpoenaed to appear in court to protect the life of a man of God who was on trial. I knew him, so I went down that day with my heart just pounding. I sat down waiting for them to call my name. But before I had the chance to testify, I saw something that I wish every man and every woman here could have seen. They were bringing up witnesses. They brought up a kind of nice looking woman. She held up her hand, and promised to tell the whole truth and nothing but the truth, and then she was told to sit down. She sat down, and the lawyer who was prosecuting said to her, "Now, what did you see on the night of October so-and-so?" She pushed back her Revlon locks and said, "Well, I think I saw—" I wish you could have been in the courtroom. The opposing attorney grabbed his hair in his hand, leaped to his feet, screamed and said, "Woman! In this courtroom, we don't say what we think. You are a witness. We speak what we know!"

Isn't that great? We are witnesses, and the Holy Spirit coming upon us makes us witnesses. "Ye shall be witnesses."

The Holy Spirit Gives Power to Communicate

Now notice Acts 2:2–4. The Holy Spirit has now come like a mighty wind and rushing sound from heaven. "And there appeared unto them cloven tongues like as of fire, and it sat upon each of them. And they were all filled with the Holy Ghost, and began to speak with other tongues, as the Spirit gave them utterance." The Holy Spirit not only came to give them power to witness, a divine enablement for witnessing, but there was also a divine enablement for communication and for utterance. Long before we got into this modern bit of communication, God moved in the lives of men in such a way on that day as to make them effective communicators. Gathered in that congregation were men out of every nation under heaven. In a few days they would be scurrying back home. They'd take Boeing jets, they'd take the Greyhound buses, some would get on their Hondas, and they'd scurry back to the cities of the ancient world. Before they left they needed to hear the message of the wonderful works of God. There came a divine enablement to the believers that gave them utterance to make the message plain, and the people heard them speak in their own language.

Now, I confess to you that the great need for this present hour is for a divine ennablement of our lives to make the message of Jesus Christ relevant, meaningful. I've had kids from our campus say, "Pastor, we don't understand these terms." Once again we need an ennablement of the Holy Spirit of God in our lives that will help us to communicate the Gospel and make the message clear and plain. This is what the Holy Spirit accomplished in the early church.

There is an interesting word in Acts 4. They prayed and in the closing part of their prayer, in verses 29–31, they said, "And now, Lord, behold their threatenings." That's the crowd outside. They were threatening, saying, "Keep your mouth shut. Don't you dare speak again about this Jesus Christ." "Now, Lord, behold their threatenings: and grant unto thy servants, that with all boldness they may speak thy word, by stretching forth thine hand to heal; and that signs and wonders may be done by the name of thy holy child Jesus. And when they had prayed, the place was shaken where they were assembled together; and they were all filled with the Holy Ghost, and they spake the word of God with boldness."

Twice in the context of their prayer and the attending results, you find the word *boldness*. Now, you miss the wonder of it if you don't realize that this word is used in another interesting passage in the New Testament in John 11. You remember the day when the boy came riding up on his bike and gave the Lord Jesus a telegram. Mary and Martha sent Him a telegram and said, "Lazarus, he whom Thou lovest, is sick. Will you please come right away?" (v. 3, author's paraphrase). And He didn't come. He talked with the disciples about it and He said, "Our friend Lazarus sleepeth" (v. 11). One of them said to another, "Well, if he's sleeping, he did better than I did last night. I took two Sominex and one Nytol and never did get to sleep all night. If Lazarus sleeps, it's good for him to sleep. What's He talking about? Why doesn't He tell us really what has happened?" And in the next verse, Jesus turned to them and said, "Lazarus is dead." They said, "Well, now, that's better. We can understand that. Now thou speakest unto us plainly" (v. 14, author's paraphrase). You know, this is the same word. The early church was meeting and they were praying one tremendous prayer like a great chorus going up to the throne of God. "O God, fill us, that we might make the Word that Thou hast given to us plain."

I was invited to a breakfast not long ago. It was really the big breakfast in our state, about a thousand businessmen came in from all over. After eating, the speaker was introduced. He spoke for thirty minutes to a thousand men. That meant five hundred hours. I had this all written down on my napkin. Five hundred hours of time at four dollars an hour. When the speaker had finished, a big businessman who sat at the next table turned to the man next to him and remarked, "What did he say?" Thirty minutes, five hundred hours of one thousand businessmen, and no one was communicated to.

Next Lord's day morning many of you will be teaching a Sunday school class. How can we stand before our classes and teach if we do not pray that in those thirty or forty-five minutes allotted to us God by His Holy Spirit will help us make our message plain. What a responsibility rests upon us; what an opportunity comes to us. The empowerment of the Holy Spirit of God in our lives is to take the Word of God and make it fit the hour in which we live. It was the need then. It is the need today.

So the Holy Spirit coming upon them made them witnesses. The Holy Spirit coming upon them gave them utterance. I like the passage in Acts that says, "They so spake that a multitude believed." The emphasis is placed upon the man, the woman, the young person who delivers the message, and it can only be delivered by divine empowerment.

The Holy Spirit Gives Good Common Sense

There is a third movement, found in Acts 6:1:

> And in those days, when the number of the disciples were multiplied, there arose a murmuring of the Grecians against the Hebrews, because their widows were neglected in the daily ministration.

There was a crisis in the church. They were headed for a healthy split between the Greeks and the Hebrews. Of course, the Hebrews were in the majority.

> Then the twelve called the multitude of the disciples unto them, and said, It is not reason [it's just not good sense] that we should leave the word of God, and serve [take care of] tables. Wherefore, brethren, look ye out among you seven men of honest report, full of the Holy Ghost and wisdom.

Williams' translation of this verse is, "Filled with the Holy Spirit and good, practical sense." When the Holy Spirit comes upon us, He will give us good common sense.

We live in days of crisis, and there are those who tell us we ought to abandon the church. This is the modern approach. We go out in little cells now and scatter all over and forget the wonder of what God is doing in the church today. Some say we ought to shift the message, and there are others who say we ought to change the music. That's wild. And then there are others who say, "No, I will take my pen and I will expose all the weaknesses of the church." Wouldn't it be great if we looked around to find men of good practical and good spiritual sense to deal with the problems? Now would you believe it, this is exactly what happened in the early church. When you look in upon this church filled with the Holy

Spirit, using good common sense, it solved many of the problems that I face as a pastor every day in my work. Notice what they did. They had a prayer meeting. "We will give ourselves continually to prayer," these men said, "and to the ministry of the word. And the saying pleased the whole multitude: and they chose Stephen, a man full of faith" (vv. 4–5). Then all the men are listed.

You know this, but isn't it good to be reminded that good, practical sense in this hour of crisis saved the church from fragmenting, saved the church from becoming a scandal in the community, saved the church from scorn of its enemies, and saved the day for the early church—just good common sense! Well, what did they do? They met together to have an election. Remember the Hebrews were in the majority, and do you know what the majority of Hebrews did? They elected all Greeks. They said, "Isn't this great? We have a chance now to use good common sense." The Spirit of God filling the believers in the local church, the visible gathering of God's people, they voted and all the Hebrews voted for Greeks. They saved the day, and we read that a great multitude in Jerusalem believed, and priests were saved, and the church was refreshed, and God's revival fires began to burn. Why? Because here were believers who in a local situation used good common sense. This will solve a lot of problems.

A fellow came to me not too long ago and said, "Do you tackle the dress problem?" "No, I don't." "Well, why?" "Good common sense will teach us how to dress." Good common sense will teach us about our conduct. Good common sense will help us in our conversations. Good common sense will permeate our entire beings if we give God the Holy Spirit a chance in our lives. You know what I do? I pray for this every morning, because there are so many days I feel so low on common sense. There are so many situations where, humanly speaking, you have to be the one to call the plays. You have to be in touch with the living God and indwelt by the Holy Spirit of God, who will give you in that hour good common sense. I am always excited about the filling of the Spirit for the great, the visible; but how about the filling of the Holy Spirit today to give me good common sense in my home where I live with Mrs. Sugden, good common sense when I meet with my board of some twenty men who look to me, good common sense when I talk with my people. Oh, Christian, you just can't imagine God being more practical, can you?

The Holy Spirit Gives Joy

Ye shall receive power, the Holy Spirit coming upon you; and you will be given power to witness in a hostile world, the world outside which is unfriendly; you will be given power of utterance to make the message relevant in the world today; you will have good common sense so that in life situations you won't collapse and go to pieces, you'll be given good practical sense. Now there is another and this would seem to culminate the great moving of the Spirit of God as He works in the lives of believers. Acts 13:50: "But the Jews stirred up the devout and honorable women, and the chief men of the city, and raised persecution against Paul and Barnabas, and expelled them out of their coasts." Rather a dark day for Paul and Barnabas. I've never been treated like that. I've never had the board rise up and say, "Pastor, you are all through and out you go," and they escort me out. I don't know what I would do. I've never had to pass through some of the experiences these early believers passed through.

As they left the city, Paul said to Barnabas, "Let's go to the corner drugstore and get some Bufferin. Brother, I've had it. I've had it!" And Barnabas said, "Paul, I was doubtful about this trip when we started. I've always questioned your teaching on guidance, and this is really the crux of it. We've come into this city and we've been faithful to God. We've preached the Word of God, and now they say. 'Out you go.'" And so they were sitting just outside the city in their Volkswagon and were talking. No, the Word says, "But they shook off the dust of their feet against them, and came unto Iconium. And the disciples were filled with joy" (v. 51).

Joy! Do you believe it? I can't believe that I could be taken and pushed to the door, and told "We don't want your message anymore. We have no patience with your teaching. Out with you!" and my heart filled with rapturous joy? I don't know, do you?

A friend of mine went to his board meeting for ten years with his resignation in his pocket. Every time the going got rough, he'd reach in his pocket, and one of the board would say, "I move we keep him." One day he was slow on the draw, and when he called me the next morning he wasn't filled with joy in the Holy Spirit.

Imagine the Holy Spirit indwelling the life of the Christian and filling the life of the Christian, making a believer in the most difficult of all circumstances to have joy in Jesus Christ. I commend to you that you take your *Young's* or *Strong's* or *Cruden's* concordance and go through the passages in Acts on the subject of joy. The word *joy* is used twenty-one times in the book. There was something about these early believers; they were joyful people, and joy, someone has said, is the echo of the life of God in the soul. Think of it, the joy of God in my soul today. You know, I have discovered some interesting things. They had the joy of fellowship in Acts 2. They had the joy of suffering in Acts 5. They had joy in prayer in Acts 12. They rejoiced that God had given them a revelation in Acts 15. Everything that broke in upon their lives gave these believers an occasion to joy.

Sometimes I've received letters from my radio audience and they say, "Pastor Sugden, we feel sometimes that you are too happy." Boy! Does that ever get me! Imagine a Christian moving through this world and climbing the steep ascent to heaven through peril, toil, and pain. He ought to be happy with the destination of heaven, hell behind him, and the Spirit of God indwelling him. I think sometimes we have severed ourselves and produced a generation gap because there has been so little joy in our spiritual lives. We go drab and monotonous and dull and ordinary. I pray to God every morning as I rise, "O Lord, save me from a rut (which is a grave with the ends knocked out). Save me from a rut of just going through life sort of drab and monotonous. No one would want what I have if I had anything." They were filled with joy in the midst of persecution.

They were witnesses. God gave them utterance. He enabled them to take the things of God and make them plain to people who so desperately needed to know what God was saying in that day. He filled them with joy, and they triumphed in the midst of circumstance.

I am a lover of preachers, and some of my preacher friends fill my shelves at home. I think I have everything that Spurgeon ever wrote. But there's another fellow who lived at the same time by the name of Theodore Cuyler. His books are exciting. On one occasion Spurgeon and Cuyler spent a holiday together. They walked along by the brooks of England and saw fish and tossed in stones, and they visited. One morning as they walked across the meadows, Cuyler told a funny story, as Cuyler could do, and Spurgeon just burst out laughing. Suddenly he stopped, and reaching out his chubby arms he took his friend in his arms and said, "Cuyler, let's get down on our knees this morning and thank God we can laugh."

Just think of it! The joy of knowing God in the circumstances of life no matter how difficult they may be—to be filled with the Holy Spirit that makes us greater than the situation we are in. That's our desire this morning. We could really sing, "Spirit of the living God, fall afresh on me." I don't want to go home the way I came. Do you? I want to go home different, and I know the desire of your heart and my heart is that the power that God has available for us with the filling of His Spirit may be ours today.

NOTES

The Work of the Spirit

Robert Murray McCheyne (1813–1843) is one of the brightest lights of the Church of Scotland. Born in Dundee, he was educated in Edinburgh and licensed to preach in 1835. In 1836 he was ordained and installed as pastor of Saint Peter's Church, Dundee, where he served until his untimely death two months short of his thirtieth birthday. He was known for his personal sanctity and his penetrating ministry of the Word, and great crowds came to hear him preach. *The Memoirs of and Remains of Robert Murray McCheyne*, by Andrew Bonar, is a Christian classic that every minister of the gospel should read.

This sermon is taken from *Additional Remains of The Rev. R. M. McCheyne*, published in Edinburgh in 1846 by William Oliphant and Co.

Robert Murray McCheyne

10

THE WORK OF THE SPIRIT

And the Spirit of God moved upon the face of the waters (Genesis 1:2).

THERE IS, PERHAPS, NO subject upon which there is greater ignorance than that of the Spirit of God. Most people in our day, if they answered truly, would say as those twelve men at Ephesus: "We have not so much as heard whether there be any Holy Ghost" (Acts 19:2). And yet, if ever you are to be saved, you must know Him, for it is all His work to bring a poor prisoner to Christ. A little boy, when dying, said: "Three persons in the Godhead. God the Father made and preserved me; God the Son came into the world and died for me; God the Holy Spirit came into my heart and made me love God and hate sin!" My dear friends, if you would die happy, you must be able to bear the same dying testimony. You know it is said by John that God is love (1 John 4:8). This is true of God the Father in His giving up His Son for sinners; this is true of God the Son in His becoming man and dying for sinners; this is true of God the Holy Spirit in His whole work in the heart of sinners. At present I wish to show you the love of the Spirit by observing all that He has ever done for men in the world. Today I will show you His work at creation, at the flood, in the wilderness.

The Holy Spirit's Work at Creation

"The Spirit of God moved upon the face of the waters" (Gen. 1:2). The expression is taken from a dove brooding over its nest. "Thou sendest forth thy Spirit, they are created: and thou renewest the face of the earth" (Ps. 104:30). Here the Spirit is said to have renewed the face of the earth. He made every blade of grass to spring, every flower to open, every tree to put forth blossoms. "By his spirit he hath garnished the heavens" (Job 26:13). Here God does, as it were, lead us forth to look upon the midnight sky. When we gaze upon its spangled maze, studded with brilliant stars, He tells us that it was the loving Spirit that gave them all their brightness and their beauty. Observe, then, that whatever beauty there is in the glassy sea, in the green earth, or in the spangled sky, it is all the work of the Holy Spirit. God the Father willed all; God the Son created all; God the Holy Spirit garnished, and gave life and loveliness to all. Oh! what a lovely world that unfallen world must have been—when God the Son walked with Adam in Paradise, when God the Holy Spirit watered and renewed the whole every moment, when God the Father looked down well pleased on all, and said that all was very good.

Learn, first, *the love of the Spirit*. He did not think it beneath His care to beautify the dwelling place of man. He wanted our joy to be full. He did not think it enough that we had a world to live in, but He made the waters full of life and beauty. He made every green thing to spring for man and made a shining canopy above, all for the joy of man. Whatever beauty still remains in earth or sea or sky, it is the trace of His almighty finger. You should never look on the beauties of the world without thinking of the Holy Spirit that moved upon the face of the waters, that renewed the face of the earth, that garnished the heavens with stars.

Second, learn *the holiness of the Spirit*. From the very beginning He was the *Holy* Spirit, of purer eyes than to behold iniquity. It was a sinless world. The sea had never been defiled by bearing wicked men upon its bosom. The green earth had never been trodden by the foot of a sinner. The spangled sky had never been looked upon by one whose eye is full of adultery and cannot cease from sin. It was a holy, holy, holy world—a temple of the living God; the lofty mountains were the pillars of it, the glittering heavens its canopy. The far-resounding ocean sang His praise. The hills brake forth into singing, and all the trees of the field clapped their hands. As the cloud so filled Solomon's temple that the priests could not stand to minister by reason of the cloud, so the Holy Spirit filled this world—a holy, sinless temple to the Father's praise. When man fell into sin, and the very ground was cursed for his sake, then the Holy Spirit, in great measure, left His temple; He could not dwell with sin. And never do you find Him coming back, as before, until He lighted on the head of a sinless Savior, for the Holy Spirit descended upon Him like a dove and abode upon Him.

Just so is it with the soul. As long as your soul is guilty, polluted, vile in the sight of the Spirit, He cannot make His abode in your heart. He is a loving Spirit, full of a tender desire to make you holy. But as long as you are guilty in His sight, it is contrary to His nature that He should dwell in you. But come to the blood of Jesus, sinner—come to the blood that makes you white as snow; then will the Spirit see no iniquity in you, and He will come and dwell in your heart, as He dwelt at first in the sinless world. As He moved on the face of the waters, like a dove over its nest, so He will make His nest in your heart and brood there. As He renewed the face of the ground, so will He renew your heart. As He garnished the heavens, so will He beautify your soul, until He make you shine as the stars forever and ever.

The Holy Spirit's Work at the Flood

"My spirit shall not always strive with man, for that he also is flesh [fading]: yet his days shall be an hundred and twenty years" (Gen. 6:3). What a different scene we have here! Yet here also we shall learn that the Holy Spirit is a loving Spirit. At the creation we found Him beautifying the world—dwelling in it as in a temple; the earth, the sea, the sky, all proclaiming that it was a sinless world. But now fifteen hundred years had passed away, and the whole earth was covered with a race of godless men—giants in body and giants in wickedness.

"God looked upon the earth, and . . . it was corrupt" (Gen. 6:12). It was all one putrid mass. "From the sole of the foot even unto the head there is no soundness in it" (Isa. 1:6); for all flesh had corrupted his way. Just as a putrid body is loathsome in the sight of man, so the earth was loathsome in the sight of God. Even more; the earth was filled with violence. The few children of God that remained were hated and persecuted—hunted like the partridge on the mountains. It repented the Lord that He had made man, and it grieved Him at His heart.

How is the Holy Spirit engaged? He does not dwell with sinful men. He cannot dwell with unpardoned sinners, for He is the Holy Spirit. But still He strives with men and strives to the very end. The men were giants in sin. Every imagination of their hearts was only evil continually. But this is the very reason He strives. He sees the flood that is coming—He sees the hell that is beneath them; therefore does He strive. In the preaching of Noah He pleaded with them; He pricked their hearts—made them think of their danger, their sin, their misery. In preparing the ark He pleaded with them—showed them the way of safety, and said: "Yet there is room." He made every stroke of the hammer speak to their hearts.

From this we learn, first, that *He is a striving Spirit.* O! let those of you that are living in sin learn what a loving Spirit is now striving with you. Some of you, who are living in sin, think that God is nothing but an angry God; therefore you do not turn to Him. True, "God is angry with the wicked every day" (Ps. 7:11); still He is striving with the wicked every day. He sends the Holy Spirit to strive with you. Oh! what a loving Spirit He is that does not at once turn you into hell, but pleads and strives, saying: "Turn ye, turn ye; . . . why will ye die?" (Ezek. 33:11).

Some may say: I am a giant in wickedness, I am corrupt, I am violent against God's children. True, yet still see here how He strove with giants in wickedness. The whole earth was corrupt and filled with violence;

yet He strove. So He strives with you in whatever state you are. He is a loving Spirit. He strives by ministers, Bibles, providences. Sometimes, when you are all alone, that Spirit wrestles with you, brings your sin to remembrance, and makes you tremble, or, like the angels at Sodom, strives to make you flee from destruction. Oh! what love is here, to strive with hell-deserving worms. Oh! "Ye stiffnecked and uncircumcised in heart and ears, ye do always resist the Holy Ghost: as your fathers did, so do ye" (Acts 7:51).

We also learn that *He is a long-suffering Spirit.* One hundred and twenty years He strove with the men before the flood. He never ceased until the flood came. Some of you remember a time when God's Spirit was striving with you at the Sabbath school or your first sacrament. You wept for your soul and prayed, but the world has come on you since then, and now you fear He strives no more. Learn, He is a long-suffering Spirit—He strives with you yet. "He that hath an ear, let him hear what the Spirit saith unto the churches" (Rev. 2:7, etc.).

We learn, too, that *He will not always strive.* Observe, the Spirit strove until the flood came, but no longer; the flood came and carried them all away. So it is with you, my dear friends. As long as our ministry lasts He strives with you, but when death comes or when the Savior comes, He will strive no more. Ah! you will have no awakening, inviting, striving sermons in hell—not one invitation more. Oh! how sad it is to think that so many who have the Spirit of God striving with them should perish after all.

The Holy Spirit's Work in the Wilderness

Nearly one thousand years after the flood, we find God choosing a peculiar people to Himself and keeping them separate from all people in the wilderness. Here the Spirit shows Himself still more as the loving Spirit.

He is the glorifier of Christ. Bezaleel and Aholiab, by His guidance, make the tabernacle—the mercy seat, the altar, the high priest's garments (Ex. 31:1–11). All these typify Christ. The Spirit here enables these men to show forth the Savior to the many thousands of Israel. Although Israel often vexed the Holy Spirit and grieved Him in the desert, yet see here how lovingly He sets forth Christ in the midst of them that He may lead them to peace and holiness! This is exactly what Christ said of Him afterward: "He shall glorify me: for he shall receive of mine, and shall shew it unto you" (John 16:14).

Dear friends, has the Spirit glorified Christ to you? He is still the great revealer of Christ. He shines into our hearts, to give us the light of the knowledge of the glory of God in the face of Christ. Has He led you to the altar—to the Lamb of God that takes away the sin of the world? Has He clothed you in the high priest's garments? Has He brought you within the veil—to the mercy seat? This is His delightful work. Oh! it is a sweet work to be the minister on earth that leads souls to Christ—that points, like John, and says: "Behold the Lamb of God" (John 1:29). But oh, how infinitely more loving in that Holy Spirit of God to lead trembling souls to Jesus! Oh! praise Him that has done this for you. Oh! love the Spirit of God. "Thy spirit is good; lead me into the land of uprightness (Ps. 143:10)."

He purifies all that believe. "Thou shalt set the laver between the tent of the congregation and the altar" (Ex. 40:7). This brazen laver, containing water, was set up in the wilderness to typify the Holy Spirit. Observe the place where it was put—between the altar and the tabernacle of God. The first thing that the sinner came up to was the altar with the bleeding lamb. He laid his hands upon the head of the lamb and confessed his sins, so that they were carried all away in the blood of the lamb. Forgiven and justified, he advanced a few paces farther to the brazen laver; there he washed his feet and hands. This represented the Holy Spirit washing and renewing his heart; then he entered into the Holy Place of God.

"Whatsoever things were written aforetime were written for our learning, that we through patience and comfort of the scripture might have hope" (Rom. 15:4). Dear friends, has the Holy Spirit purified you? If you have laid your sins upon the Lamb of God, have you come to this laver of living water? Are you really washing there and preparing to enter into the Holy Place made without hands, eternal in the heavens? Without holiness no man can see the Lord (see Heb. 12:14), and without the Spirit you will have no holiness. Oh! is He not a loving Spirit who thus delights to prepare the believer for glory, who comes into our vile hearts, and creates a clean heart, and renews a right spirit within us? Oh! love Him who thus loves you, and ask for Him, you that are His children. The Father delights to give Him. "If ye then, being evil, know how to give good gifts unto your children: how much more shall your heavenly Father give the Holy Spirit to them that ask him?" (Luke 11:13).

He upholds the life of believers. "They drank of that spiritual Rock that followed them: and that Rock was Christ" (1 Cor. 10:4). This was a third way in which the Spirit showed Himself in the wilderness.

1. *A river.* This was to show Israel how refreshing and supporting He is to the weary soul and that there is abundance in Him. Drink, and drink again—you will not drink a river dry; so there is infinite fullness of the Spirit.
2. *Flowing from a smitten rock.* This shows that He is given by a wounded Savior—that it is only when we hide in that Rock that we can receive the Holy Spirit. "I will send him unto you" (John 16:7).
3. *It followed them.* This was to show that wherever a believer goes, the Holy Spirit goes with him: "I will pray the Father, and he will give you another Comforter, that he may abide with you for ever" (John 14:16)—a well within, springing up into everlasting life.

My dear friends, have you received the Holy Spirit since you believed? It appears to me that few Christians realize this river flowing after them. Oh! what inexpressible love and grace there is in this work of the Spirit. Is there any of you weak and faint and ready to perish under a wicked heart and raging lusts? Have you gotten a thorn in the flesh—a messenger of Satan to buffet you? Are you driven to pray that it may be taken from you? See here the answer to your prayer. A river of living water flows from Christ. There is enough here for all your wants: "My grace is sufficient for thee: for my strength is made perfect in weakness" (2 Cor. 12:9). Some of you are afraid of the future—you fear some approaching temptation, you fear some coming contest. See here the river flows after you—the Spirit will abide with you forever. Oh! what love is here. Notwithstanding all your sinfulness and weakness and unbelief, still He abides with you and will forever. He is "a well of water springing up into everlasting life" (John 4:14).

Oh! love the Spirit, then, who so loves you. Grieve not the Holy Spirit of God, whereby you are sealed unto the day of redemption.

NOTES

The Holy Spirit Our Teacher

Joseph Barber Lightfoot (1828–1889) is best known today as a Greek scholar and the author of erudite commentaries on Paul's epistles, but he was also a gifted preacher and teacher. After ministering in various posts in the Anglican Church, he served as professor at Cambridge and in 1879 was ordained bishop of Durham, a position he filled with distinction until his death. He served for ten years on the revision committee for the English Revised Version of the New Testament. Lightfoot had both a scholar's mind and a pastor's heart and was very conscientious in preparing men for ordination.

This message is taken from his book *Ordination Addresses and Counsels to Clergy*, published posthumously in 1891 by Macmillan and Company, London.

Joseph Barber Lightfoot

11

THE HOLY SPIRIT OUR TEACHER

> He will guide you into all Truth. . . . He shall take of Mine, and shall shew it unto you (John 16:13–14, translation mine).

THIS IS THE LAST evening that we shall spend together. Once again we meet—tomorrow morning—for our farewell service, when I hope to address to you a very few parting words. But so far as regards these meditations, this is the close.

How then can I more faithfully fulfill my part than by striving to lead you into the presence of the Eternal Guide Himself and there leave you! There are tutors many and various. It is a high privilege for any of us to be called to fulfill this function, however mean our capacities and however poor the fulfillment. But there is one only Teacher, the Eternal Spirit of Truth, who takes of the things of Christ and shows them to us.

The death of Christ threatened to be the orphanhood of the disciples. I need not tell you that where our English Bibles make Him speak of leaving them comfortless, His own expression is "leave you desolate, leave you orphans." They would be fatherless, motherless, homeless, friendless—at least so it seemed to them—when He was gone. Their natural guardian, teacher, friend would be withdrawn. They would be left as waifs and strays on the ocean of this life—swept to and fro by the tide of human affairs, to be stranded no one could say where.

Who shall say that this was an exaggeration of their hopeless state at this crisis? They had left all and followed Him. They had forsaken parents and friends, and He had become father and mother and sister and brother to them. They had surrendered houses and lands, and

He was henceforth their home. Their dependence on Him was absolute. Whatever of joy they had in the present and whatever of hope they cherished for the future were alike centered in Him.

And now this close communion of soul with soul and of life with life must be ruthlessly severed. Christ slain, Christ buried, Christ lost—lost forever as it would seem to them—what joy, what strength, what comfort could they have henceforward? Surely never was orphanhood more helpless, more hopeless, than the orphanhood of these poor Galileans!

The Teacher

It was to prepare them for this terrible trial that the promise in the text was given. *He* must go, but another should come. They should not be without a teacher, without a guide. One Paraclete, one Counselor, one Advocate, should be withdrawn, but another should take His place. There would still be a friend, an adviser, ever near to take them by the hand, to whisper into their ear, to prompt, to instruct, to protect, to fortify, to guide them into all truth.

Another Paraclete, yet not another. There would not be less of Christ, but more of Christ, when Christ was gone. This is the spiritual paradox which is assured to the disciples by the promise in the text, "He shall take of Mine, and shall shew it unto you. All things that the Father hath are Mine: therefore said I, that He shall take of Mine, and shall shew it unto you" (John 16:14–15, translation mine).

Another, and yet not another. It was not Christ supplanted, not Christ superseded, not Christ eclipsed and quenched, but a larger, higher, truer, more abundant Christ with whom henceforward they should live, a Christ whose tongue was ever articulate, though no waves of air might vibrate with the impulse. It was not a Christ of now or then, not a Christ of here or there, but a Christ of every moment and in every place, a Christ as permeating as the Spirit is permeating, for He is wafted on the wings of the Spirit, whithersoever the Spirit finds an entrance. He shall take of Mine, and shall show it unto you. "Lo, I am with you alway"—I and not another—"even unto the end of the world" (Matt. 28:20).

The compensation was more than a compensation. It was even expedient that Christ should go away. The effect on the temper of the disciples is immediate. On the eve of the severance they are weak, hesitating, fearful, sense-bound and narrow in their ideas. On the morrow they are strong, steadfast, courageous, far-sighted, endowed with a new spiritual faculty, which pierces into the heaven of heavens. If hitherto they have known Christ after the flesh, henceforth they will know Him so no more.

To have known Christ after the flesh—what would we not give to have known Christ after the flesh! What a source of strength it would have been to us just to have listened to one of those parables spoken by His own lips, just to have witnessed one of those miracles of healing wrought by His own hands, just to have looked, if it were only for a moment, on Him as He stood silent in the judgment hall or hung bleeding on the cross! So we persuade ourselves foolishly.

To have known Christ after the flesh—what would such knowledge have profited us? Did not all the disciples who forsook Him and fled know Him after the flesh? Did not Thomas who doubted and Peter who denied know Him after the flesh? Did not Judas who betrayed and Caiaphas who plotted and Herod who scorned and Pilate who condemned know Him after the flesh? Did not the Jewish mob that hooted and reviled and the Roman soldiers who mocked and scourged know Him after the flesh? What security was this knowledge after the flesh against skepticism, against cowardice, against blasphemy, against apostasy and rebellion? Seeing, it is said, is believing; yes, and hearing too. But it is the seeing of the spiritual eye, and the hearing of the spiritual ear; the seeing of a Stephen, when he beheld the heavens open and the Son of Man standing at the right hand of God; the hearing of a Paul, when he was caught up into Paradise and heard unspeakable words which it is not lawful for a man to utter.

This then is the function of the Spirit as described by our Lord Himself in the text. To us, as to the disciples of old, the Spirit offers not less but more of Christ. In place of a Christ who walked on the shores of a Galilean lake, who sat down weary on the brink of a Samaritan well, who shed tears over a doomed city on the brow of Olivet—instead of such a Christ, or rather through such a Christ, He presents to us a Christ of all times and in all places, a Christ whose throne is the heaven, and the earth is His footstool, a Christ who traverses the universe.

Look at the explanation that is attached to the promise. He shall take of *Mine*, and shall show it unto you. How so? Why of Christ's, and Christ's only? Has the Spirit nothing else to teach? Hear what follows: "All things that the Father hath are mine: therefore said I, that he shall take of mine, and shall shew it unto you" (John 16:15). So again at a later point; "All mine are thine, and thine are mine." All things—there is no limitation—all history, all science, all creation, all truth in whatever domain it may be. "Think you," He seems to say to us, "think you that My working is confined to a few paltry miracles wrought in Galilee? The universe itself is My miracle. Think you that My words are restricted to a few short precepts uttered to the Jews? Heaven and earth are vocal with My teaching."

We make our foolish distinctions, we impose our artificial limitations, we confine the Christ of our imagining within narrow barriers of our erecting, but Christ, the Christ of Christ's own teaching, the Christ of the Spirit's showing, overleaps all barriers. We are careful to distinguish between natural and revealed religion. We exclude our Christ from the former, and we relegate Him to the latter, but the Christ of Christ's own teaching is the Eternal Word, through whom the Father speaks, whensoever and wheresoever He speaks. We draw a rigid line between science and theology, between religion and nature, but the Christ of the Bible is the hand of the Father not less in science and nature than in religion and theology. We have our trenchant distinctions between the secular and the spiritual, as if the two were directly antagonistic or at least reciprocally exclusive. We misinterpret a saying of Christ, as if it taught that our duty to Caesar was something quite apart from our duty to God; as if forsooth it were possible to have any moral obligation to any man or any body of men that was not also an obligation to God in Christ. But the Christ of the Gospels claims sovereignty over all alike—over that which we call secular not less than over that which we call spiritual. "All things that the Father hath are mine: therefore said I, that he shall take of mine."

The Lesson

And so we pass by a natural transition from the Teacher to the lesson—the all-pervading, all-comprehensive lesson, which centers in the incarnation of the Divine Word.

We cannot afford in this nineteenth century to restrict either the operations of the Teacher or the bearings of the lesson. Human knowledge, human thought, human interest, has expanded on all sides to an extent almost without a parallel in the history of our race. We are constrained to ask what relation all this has to our theological conceptions, to our religious aspirations? Least of all can you, who as teachers at a great university are brought across all currents of thought and knowledge, afford to be indifferent to this wider teaching of the Spirit. You will strive, so far as you may, to take all these lessons up into Christ. You will do your little—it may not be much—to solve the enigmas that they present. You will not be impatient. You are finite, and the lessons are infinite. But at all events you will recognize the problem in its breadth and magnitude. You will at least reject the distinctions of popular religion and take your stand once more on the teaching of the apostles.

I remember once hearing a sermon from a very famous man on the doctrine of the Trinity. He told his hearers that the First Person of the Blessed Trinity was God in Nature, and the Second was God in Revelation. This is just the heresy against which I am contending put into its most epigrammatic form. This is the very negation—though the preacher saw it not—of the teaching of the apostles. For what does Paul mean when he tells us that by Him and for Him, through Him and to Him all things were created, things visible, as well as things invisible, things in heaven as well as things on earth? What does John mean when he tells us that by Him all things were made and without Him has not anything been made; that He was in the world from the beginning, though the world knew Him not? What does the writer to the Hebrews mean when he describes Him as upholding all things, the whole universe, by the Word of His power? No, what does Christ Himself mean when He affirms, "All things that the Father hath are mine"?

So then to you who are disciples of the Logos, the great central fact of Christianity will have this wider meaning. You, like Paul, will determine to know nothing but Jesus Christ and Him crucified—the incarnation of the Word culminating in the passion—but you will know it in all its manifold bearings. You will not be content to regard it, as it is too commonly regarded, in one narrow relation, from one cramped and confined point of view. It will be to you the center of all your moral and all your theological aspirations. For what does it proclaim? Nothing less than the absolute righteousness and the infinite love of God—the absolute righteousness not only in the manifestation of a faultless exemplar of a perfect human life, but still more in the stupendous sacrifice of the Incarnation and the Cross.

And where again is God's fatherly goodness and love so manifested as in the incarnation and passion of Christ? He, who from all eternity was in the form of God, holds it not beneath Him to take upon Himself the form of a man, the form of a slave. Try to realize this fact. It is a thought that transcends all thinking. Summon to your aid all the analogies that history can supply or imagination can invent. They all fade into nothingness before the condescension of the love of Christ. Before the eternal throne, the mightiest prince and the meanest beggar are as one. The infinite distance annihilates our petty distinctions between one human littleness and another, the littleness of an Alexander or a Napoleon and the littleness of the veriest pauper wasted with famine and disease. To the ruler of the universe it were as much an act of condescension to become an emperor as to become a peasant, to wield the scepter of an Augustus as to ply the tools in the carpenter's shop at Nazareth. Yet for our sakes He preferred the meaner alternative.

And what did He gain by this condescension? Was it popularity or honor or gratitude? He was reviled; He was misunderstood; He was despised and rejected; He had no where to lay His head. He was condemned as the lowest criminal; He was gibbeted—He, the Lord of heaven and earth, was gibbeted amid the acclamations of a ruthless mob and a ribald soldiery. Yes, herein was love, herein, if anywhere, not that we loved Him (did we not hate Him, did we not persecute Him, did we not kill Him?). Herein was love, that while we were yet sinners, while we were yet rebels, Christ died for us.

But, as you are disciples not only of the incarnate Christ but of the eternal Logos, this great fact of the Incarnation will have wider application for you. The old perplexing question, "What is the origin of evil?" will still remain. It is far older than the Christian revelation. The mystery of sin and death is yet unsolved, until we know even as we are known. But the Christian revelation at least offers us a corrective. Once you realize the Incarnation and the Cross of Christ as the manifestation of the Father's love, you can afford to wait patiently. All must become clear in His good time.

"He shall take of mine." Are we attracted by the magnificent discoveries in science which are the special glory of our age? Do these discoveries appeal at once to our imagination as fairy tales, and to our reason as logical demonstrations? Has Christ then—our Christ—

no handiwork in these? No, if the apostles be true, it was He—the same Christ who lay in the manger at Bethlehem and hung on the cross at Calvary—He Himself who hurled the planets into space, He Himself who charged the air with electricity, He Himself who stored up coals for fuel and stones for building countless ages before man trod this earth. We speak commonly of the "revelations" of science. Revelations indeed they are—not merely of inanimate processes, not merely of impersonal laws, but revelations of the eternal Word, through whom the Father works. Therefore as Christians we are bound to look upon these as Christ's. Therefore, if we are true to our heavenly schooling, the Spirit will take also of these and will show them to us.

"He shall take of mine." Are we diligent students of the lessons of history? Do we delight to trace the progress of the human race from the first dawn of civilization to its noonday blaze; to decipher the obscure past of the great nations of the earth in their language and their institutions; to mark the development of the arts of government; to follow the ever-widening range of intellectual thought; to discern everywhere the stream of human life broadening slowly down with the course of the ages? Then let us see the finger of Christ not less in the progress of history than in the laws of science. "He was in the world, . . . and the world knew him not" (John 1:10). He was the true Light, which lighteth every man," the light burning ever brighter and clearer through the ages until it attained its full glory in the Incarnation. The school of human history also is a school of the Holy Spirit, for it is a setting forth of Christ.

"He shall take of mine." If you have traced Christ's footprints in the processes of nature, if you have heard Christ's voice in the teachings of history, then surely you will not fail to see and to hear Him in your domestic and social relations. That pure affection which has been to you a perennial fountain of benediction, that ennobling friendship which has been a crown of glory to your life—can you, dare you, think of it apart from Christ? If you find not Christ here, assuredly you will seek Him in vain elsewhere. What was that nobility, that truthfulness, that purity, that unselfishness, that devotion, which attracted you, but a broken light of the great Light, a reflected ray from the central Sun Himself? Yes; the Spirit took of Christ's and showed it to you, when through that affection, through that friendship, He held up to you a nobler, because a more Christlike, ideal of life, shaming you out of your baser self.

"He shall take of Mine." "He shall . . . bring all things to your remembrance, whatsoever I have said unto you" (John 14:26). Last and chiefest—for this is the crown of all the other teaching, this gives their force, their meaning, to all the other lessons—He shall set before you the full significance of those unique words and works of Christ, the words not less operative than the works, the works not less articulate than the words. He shall lead you to understand, to apply, to extend them to all the varying needs of your daily life. He shall teach you the lesson of the Incarnation. He was made Man. He shall teach you the lesson of the passion. He shall remind you day and night of the paramount obligation that it lays upon you—"thou, yes *thou*, art bought with a price: thou art not thine own" (1 Cor. 6:19–20, author's paraphrase)—until the love of Christ shall constrain you wholly, shall bind you hand and foot, shall lead you captive to the will of God. He shall teach you the lesson of the Resurrection, shall lead you to know, as Paul desired to know, the power of that Resurrection, emancipating, purifying, strengthening, exalting, until He makes you conformable thereunto.

Thus you too will rise from the sepulcher in which you have lain many days, will cast off the graveclothes of inveterate evil habit, will breathe the pure air of God's presence once more, will sit at meat with your risen Lord. Though in the world, you will no longer be of the world. Despite all the environments of the senses and all the disabilities of weakness, you will live even now as full citizens of that kingdom of heaven, which is righteousness and peace and joy in the Holy Spirit.

The Wind of the Spirit

James S. Stewart (1896–1990) pastored three churches in Scotland before becoming professor of theology at the University of Edinburgh (1936) and then professor of New Testament (1946). But he was a professor who preached, a scholar who applied biblical truth to the needs of common people, and a theologian who made doctrine practical and exciting. He published several books of lectures and biblical studies including *A Man in Christ* and *Heralds of God*. His two finest books of sermons are *The Gates of New Life* and *The Strong Name*.

This sermon is taken from *The Wind of the Spirit*, published in 1968 by Abingdon Press.

James S. Stewart

12
THE WIND OF THE SPIRIT

> The wind bloweth where it listeth, and thou hearest the sound thereof, but canst not tell whence it cometh, and whither it goeth: so is every one that is born of the Spirit (John 3:8).

TO ANYONE BROUGHT UP in the Jewish tradition, it was natural, almost inevitable, to compare the Spirit of God with the wind. For in the Hebrew tongue the same term was used for both. The word *ruach* stood in fact for three things. It meant breath, that most impalpable part of existence, the breath of life. It meant also the desert wind, tearing violently across the land with primal energy and elemental force. And it meant the Spirit of God, the supernatural power that sweeps across the ages and bursts into history and takes possession of the lives of men.

Now here was Jesus with Nicodemus on the Mount of Olives. It was night, with the moon riding high above Jerusalem and driven clouds scudding across the face of the moon. The wind blowing up from the valley was stirring the branches and rustling the leaves of the olive trees. Jesus was speaking to Nicodemus about the work of God in the soul and the new birth—how God could take a life that was conscious of failure and emptiness and dissatisfaction and sin, and transform it and make it full and strong and vital and victorious. But Nicodemus was not understanding. He—a master in Israel, a theologian and an accredited leader—found this kind of talk beyond him. So Jesus took an illustration. And Jesus did not need to search far for His illustration that night. It was there, asking to be used. "Listen to the wind, Nicodemus! Listen to the wind! You can hear its sound—the night is full of it, hark to it in the tops of the trees—

but where it has come from and where it is going no man knows. Now, Nicodemus, the Spirit of God is just like that: invisible yet unmistakable, impalpable yet full of power, able to do wonderful things for you if only you will stand in its path and turn your face to it and open your life to its influence. Just listen to the wind, Nicodemus! Listen to the wind!"

Now what is Jesus saying here to us? We will break this text up into its component parts, and see.

The Ceaseless Action of the Spirit

First, this. "The wind bloweth." That bare, simple statement affirms the ceaseless action of the Spirit. This indeed is the basic fact of life. Never has there been a time, never a moment, when the Spirit of God has not been actively at work.

Look at the Bible. It is there on the first page. "The Spirit of God moved upon the face of the waters" (Gen. 1:2): the Lord God brooding over the chaos that was to become a world. It is there on the last page. "I am . . . the bright and morning star. And the Spirit and the bride say, Come" (Rev. 22:16–17). So from the beginning of days to the last syllable of recorded time, the wind blows—the Spirit of God is at work. "Whither shall I go from thy spirit?" cries a psalmist (Ps. 139:7). I can ascend to heaven, and He is there. I can make my bed in hell, and He is there. I can take the wings of the morning or hide in midnight—but He is there (see Ps. 139:7–11). God never lets go. If God did let go of this universe for an instant, if God withdrew the action of His Spirit, the whole complicated structure would disintegrate and fly apart—like a shattered mirror—into a million fragments. It is the Spirit who holds human life together. Never does He cease working. The wind blows.

Of course, the New Testament goes beyond this. The New Testament says that at one particular point of history there was a sudden new irruption of the Spirit into human life. Jesus, in whom the whole power of the divine Spirit had been focused, had died and risen from the dead in the mightiest of all the Spirit's mighty acts; now, upon the church that called Him Lord, there burst the mighty rushing wind of Pentecost. In other words, those people felt the sudden start and shock of being possessed by the identical power that had been in Jesus and was now and forever inseparable from Jesus. And still from that moment to this, "the wind bloweth"—sometimes a gentle zephyr, sometimes a judgment hurricane, sometimes a quiet guiding voice in the hour of meditation, sometimes a fierce tornado casting down strongholds of the powers of darkness in the name of Christ—always the Spirit of God at work!

No doubt, there have been times when men have been heard lamenting that God had deserted His creation and left it to its own confused, corrupt devices; times when, in faith's eclipse, Elijah's scathing words about Baal seemed almost applicable to the Lord of heaven—"Cry aloud, for he is a god" (1 Kings 18:27). Either he is musing, or he is on a journey, or perhaps he is asleep and must be awakened. "God sits in heaven and does nothing," grumbled Thomas Carlyle. And H. G. Wells in his last testament, which he called "Mind at the end of its tether," declared man to be played out, the world jaded and devoid of recuperative power, and the only possible philosophy a stoical cynicism. Some of us may have felt like that about our own lives occasionally. "Where is the blessedness I knew when first I saw the Lord? My soul is at the end of its tether—I have nothing to show but the shabby rags and tatters of my mistakes. There is no rebirth nor refreshing anywhere for me." Some are feeling like that about the church: Where is the hope of revival now? But—listen to the wind, Nicodemus! Listen to the wind, Carlyle and Wells and all you pessimists and cynics! And O my defeated and discomfited soul, listen to the wind, the music of the dawn wind of Easter and Pentecost! Bless the Lord that through all the chaos of the world, through all the complexities of your own life, God's Spirit is forever active. On that fact depends all our hope and expectation. In the blackest night, if you open the windows and listen, you will hear the wind and know that God is stirring, never slumbering, never resting, never desisting from His work of providence and redemption; His cosmic patience is the salvation of the world.

The Sovereign Freedom of the Spirit

Second: "the wind bloweth *where it listeth.*" If the first affirmation was the ceaseless action of the Spirit, this is the sovereign freedom of the Spirit. Just as it is impossible to control the wind or dictate to it its direction, so no man, no church, can domesticate the Spirit of God or delimit His sphere of operation.

Men have always wanted to do that. They have drawn their rigid dividing lines and said, "Here is the area in which grace will be valid—in this church, this sect, this racial group, this method of evangelism, this pattern of mission, this old-time religion, this newest of new theologies. Outside this sphere, no salvation!"

This is the perennial temptation of institutional religion. In fact, it is the temptation of all our work for Christ: to imagine that our way of doing things in the kingdom of Christ is the one and only way and to be impatient of every other.

But God is forever upsetting our neat logical schemes and discomfiting our tidy regulations.

Watch how it happened in Jesus' day. Judaism said: "We are the covenant people. We will have no truck with Gentiles and barbarians and lesser breeds without the law. No salvation outside Israel!" And they stood there doggedly and built high and strong their wall of partition. And then one day, out of the darkness of Mount Calvary, from the red dawn of an empty tomb, there arose a great wind of the Spirit that battered on that wall and leveled it to the dust. With a crash that startled the world the wall of exclusion went down like matchwood before the gale of Pentecost.

There are men working overtime to rebuild it today with their policies of segregation and their monopolies of grace. Let them beware! The wall will go down again before the tornado of the truth of Christ, and it may bury beneath its ruins those who try to build it.

Always that elusive and intractable Spirit of God keeps embarrassing our preconceptions. For example: why should Rahab the harlot find a place in the great panorama of Hebrews 11 and in the ancestry of Jesus Christ? Surely, we protest, that line should have been preserved impeccable! Why should Christianity offer the world an image of God all mixed up with a carpenter's bench and a wayside gallows, this appallingly unphilosophical "scandal of particularity"? Why should providence bypass Athens and Rome and Alexandria and locate the Savior of the world in the drab provincialism of Nazareth—can any good thing come out of Nazareth? Or pass down the centuries. What a shameful thing, cried the prim sticklers for ecclesiastical etiquette of John Wesley's day, what an utterly disreputable thing, to cheapen religion by carrying it outside the church walls where it belonged and defiling it in the common concourse of the streets! Rank heresy!

But that is God's way. "The wind bloweth"—not where we timidly suggest or dogmatically demand that it should, not where the most up-to-date computer decrees—"where it listeth." Try shutting the door against it, setting your shoulder to the door and barricading it—and it will break the door down, as on the day when they rolled a great massive stone against the mouth of a tomb in a garden and sealed it fast and said, "That's Christ finished! This dead and defeated man will trouble us no more. Let him sleep behind the stone forever!" Suddenly came the wind of heaven and burst the tomb, and Christ went conquering through the world.

Don't try to tame that intractable wind. No act of convocation or assembly can circumscribe it, no arrogant political dictator curb it, no rooted personal prejudice patronize it. It is master of the world.

And—don't you see?—this is the essential optimism of Christianity. Here in the Spirit of Christ is a force capable of bursting into the hardest paganism, discomfiting the most rigid dogmatism, electrifying the most suffocating ecclesiasticism.

This is the sovereign freedom of the Holy Spirit. There is no citadel of self and sin that is safe from Him, no unbelieving cynic secure beyond His reach. There is no ironclad bastion of theological self-confidence that is immune, no impregnable agnosticism He cannot disturb into faith, no ancient ecclesiastical animosities He cannot reconcile. And blessed be His name, there is no winter death of the soul that He cannot quicken into a blossoming springtime of life, no dry bones He cannot vitalize into a marching army. This is the glory of Pentecost. "The wind bloweth where it listeth." Come, Holy Spirit, come!

The Indisputable Evidence of the Spirit

Third: "the wind bloweth where it listeth, *and thou hearest the sound thereof.*" This is the indisputable evidence of the Spirit. When the wind is blowing, it makes its presence felt. You hear its sound. You do not need a lecture on the dynamics of atmospherics to tell you that something is going on. That is palpable, unmistakable.

So with the work of the Spirit. When the Spirit of God stirs up a church or an individual or a community, there are palpable evidences of His working. Even the unbeliever becomes aware that something is going on. He sees the effects. He hears its sound.

This indeed is what had brought Nicodemus to Jesus at the first. Nicodemus was not a disciple. He was a Pharisee. He belonged to a group that was naturally antipathetic to Jesus and biased against the Gospel. But he was an honest man, who kept his ears open, and he had heard the wonderful things that were happening wherever Jesus went. That is written here into the story. "Rabbi," he exclaims, "no man could do these mighty works you do unless God were with him" (John 3:2, author's paraphrase). In other words, although Nicodemus knew little or nothing about the dynamics of the messianic revival then stirring Palestine, at least he had heard its sound. He recognized the indisputable evidences. And it was that recognition which, leading him to seek an interview with Jesus, was the first step in his salvation.

Look at it again on the larger scale of the apostolic age. The hard supercilious pagan world of Greece and Rome professed itself indifferent to the Gospel, but it could not deny that wherever Christ's men went strange things kept happening. The true life of those Christians was indeed, as Paul declared, a hidden life. "Your life is hid with Christ in God" (Col. 3:3). But it was not all hidden, No! Unconcealed and open were the Christians' impact on society, their revolutionary ethic, their amazing courage amid the vicissitudes of life, their absolute serenity face-to-face with death. The world, says the book of Acts, saw the evidences: it "took knowledge of them, that they had been with Jesus" (Acts 4:13).

Always there are unmistakable signs when the power of the Spirit goes to work. "Thou hearest the sound thereof." When a man once weak and shifty and unreliable becomes strong and clean and victorious; when a church once stagnant and conventional and introverted throws off its dull tedium and catches fire and becomes alert and missionary-minded; when Christians of different denominations begin to realize there is far more in the risen Christ to unite them than there can be anywhere else in the world or in their own traditions to divide them; when religion, too long taboo in polite conversation, becomes a talking point again; when decisions for Christ are seen worked out in family and business relationships; when mystic vision bears fruit in social passion—then indeed the world is made to know that something is happening. Something vital is going on. And it is not romanticizing to say that we can thank God that all around us in these days the evidences are so indisputably clear. "The wind bloweth where it listeth, and thou hearest the sound thereof." If you have heard that sound, as I hope you have, you can refute all the minimizing and depreciating voices in your own heart and in the world around. It is the unanswerable argument for Christ.

The Inscrutable Origin of the Spirit

Fourth: "thou hearest the sound thereof, *but canst not tell whence it cometh.*" This is the inscrutable origin of the Spirit.

We all feel a certain element of mystery even in the physical wind. We cannot tell across what immense tracts of land and ocean it has made its way, nor in what atmospheric upheavals it took its birth.

So with all great movements of the Spirit. Where have they sprung from? Can you track down the factors that brought them into being? The church, the body of Christ, did that really begin as a committee meeting in Jerusalem, with Peter in the chair, appointing subcommittees to draw up a constitution? The conversion of Saul of Tarsus at the gates of Damascus—can that be represented, as some would have us believe, simply in terms of sunstroke or epilepsy or neurosis or brainwashing psychology? When Peter made his great confession of messiahship, was Jesus just being mythical when He replied, Flesh and blood have not revealed it to you, but My Father in heaven: it came to you out of eternity? Where did the Wesleyan movement begin? Was it in the rectory at Epworth? Or in the Holy Club at Oxford? Or in the meeting house in Aldersgate Street in London? These are only very partial answers. Better say it began far back in the counsels of eternity—"thou canst not tell whence."

But some do not like having to make that admission. Some want to eliminate the element of mystery and the dimension of transcendence. They would prefer to have the Father in heaven image replaced by a statement about human self-awareness. Perhaps Nicodemus himself had something of this temperament. He wanted everything explained. He was a theologian who came near losing the living God behind the abstractions of academic debate—not an unknown occurrence even today. "How can a man be born [again] when he is old?" asked Nicodemus. "Can he enter second time into his mother's womb?" (John 3:4)—Tell me precisely how this rebirth happens. It was not that Nicodemus was insincere. He just wanted a rational explanation. Where did regeneration come from?

So we rationalize and psychologize and demythologize—until the Christian faith has ceased to be good news about a living personal God acting in history and has become merely something about man and his nature, his so-called authentic existence; until theology has lost itself in anthropology; until perhaps we reach the point of the self-confident journalist who wrote, "We now know there is no such thing as the supernatural." How astonishingly naive! How frightfully callow! As if there were nothing more in this world than our logic could measure or our intelligence explore! As if man's self-awareness were the soul and center of the universe! Jesus here says to us, as He said to Nicodemus—Stop explaining, and worship! Stop arguing, and adore. What you have to do is not to tell whence the wind comes—that you will never know. What you have to do is to get your sails up to it, now that it is there; not elaborately to expound its mysterious dynamics, but gladly to yield to its living power. This is the one thing that matters. This is the appeal of Jesus, and this the challenge of Pentecost.

The Incalculable Destiny of the Spirit

Fifth and finally: "thou canst not tell whence it cometh, *and whither it goeth.*" This is the incalculable destiny of the Spirit. You cannot tell where He is liable to carry you.

The gale that blows across the earth in days of storm drives on into the unknown. And no man can tell where the Spirit of God in Christian discipleship may lead him before his life on earth is done.

Here was Nicodemus. Nicodemus did not know that night that the wind of the Spirit was going to carry him one day—do you remember where? To Pontius Pilate's council chamber to claim the body of Jesus—one of the boldest actions in the Gospel story—and beyond that to the world-shattering event of the Resurrection. The little group in the upper room at Pentecost did not know that the wind of the Spirit that was shaking them was going to carry them and their descendants to the presence of Caesar and the conquest of the world. The monk Martin Luther pondering the epistle to the Romans did not know that the wind of the Spirit stirring in his monastery cell was going to carry him to the revolutionizing and remaking of the church. And today, Christendom with two thousand years behind it does not know where the wind of the Spirit is going to carry it in the next two thousand or twenty thousand years—to what new strength of unity, what triumphs of mission, what redeeming impact on the total life of man. And for the individual—for each of us today—this incalculable destiny of the Spirit stretches out before us.

In some ways it is a daunting, even frightening thought. Perhaps some of us would think twice before praying for the gift of the Spirit if we knew where He was liable to lead us. The Spirit comes on a young man, a medical student who has just taken a brilliant university degree and seems all set to become in the course of the years a consultant at the top of his profession—the Spirit disrupts his plans for a career and sends him out as a medical missionary to Africa on a miserable pittance. The Spirit comes on a young woman immersed in the ordinary, innocent pleasures of life, and she begins to feel constrained to witness for Christ in shop or factory, university or social set. The Spirit comes upon a church proud of its venerable past, justifying itself by its meritorious history, and compels that church to take seriously the radical word of Jesus—He who saves his life shall lose it; and he who loses his life for My sake—and that includes the church that is prepared to lose its life—shall find it (Matt. 10:39). It is a daunting thought, this incalculable destiny.

But it is thrilling too. For you see, it means you just cannot tell what God may yet make of your life and character. The one thing you must never say is—My course is fixed and set and circumscribed: no chance of anything fine or noble now for me! Never—unless you are prepared to make God a liar—never under any circumstances say that. It is so atrociously untrue. For Christ at Pentecost, and every day, is holding out marvelous prospects for everyone—all the drabness and tedium vanquished, all the suffocating poisonous atmosphere of disillusionment gone with the wind of His refreshing grace. And this is not all. For beyond the hopes of earth gleams the incalculable destiny of the hereafter. "Now are we the sons of God, and it doth not yet appear what we shall be: but we know that, when he shall appear, we shall be like him; for we shall see him as he is" (1 John 3:2).

If only we would take Christ at His word today! If only the church, if each of us, would allow the Holy Spirit to have His way with us! I know the difficulties. I know all too well the towering, formidable difficulties. But I also know that in the last resort it is as simple as this: will I take Jesus at His word? Now is the accepted time. Listen to the wind, Nicodemus. Listen to the wind!

> And so the shadows fall apart,
> And so the west winds play;
> And all the windows of my heart
> I open to Thy day.

Additional Sermon Resources

Great Women of the Bible Clarence E. Macartney
A collection of sermons from a master pulpiteer of yesterday. Macartney's unique descriptive style brings these women of the Bible to life and provides inspirational reading for all Christians.

ISBN 0-8254-3268-5 **208 pp.** paperback

The Greatest Questions of the Bible and of Life Clarence E. Macartney
Discussing such questions as What shall I do with Jesus? What must I do to be saved? If a man dies, shall he live again? and Barabbas or Jesus? Clarence E. Macartney challenges his readers to ask questions and seek the answers from the pages of Holy Scripture and employ this method of teaching in his or her own situation to great profit.

ISBN 0-8254-3273-1 **192 pp.** paperback

Greatest Texts of the Bible Clarence E. Macartney
This collection of sermons represents some of the author's strongest and most impassioned preaching. Except for slight modifications and updating, and the insertion of Scripture references where needed, these sermons are reissued in their original form.

ISBN 0-8254-3266-9 **208 pp.** paperback

The Greatest Words in the Bible and in Human Speech Clarence E. Macartney
A group of fifteen sermons based on fifteen words from men's speech and their corresponding biblical meaning and significance. Macartney explores such words as: sin, forgiveness, now, whisperer, tomorrow, why, repent, heaven, memory, prayer, death, and experience.

ISBN 0-8254-3271-5 **192 pp.** paperback

He Chose Twelve Clarence E. Macartney
This careful study of the New Testament illuminates the personality and individuality of each of the Twelve Disciples. A carefully crafted series of Bible character sketches including chapters on all the apostles as well as Paul and John the Baptist.

ISBN 0-8254-3270-7 **176 pp.** paperback

Paul the Man Clarence E. Macartney
Macartney delves deeply into Paul's background and heritage, helping twentieth-century Christians understand what made him the pivotal figure of New Testament history. Paul, the missionary and theologian, are carefully traced in this insightful work.

ISBN 0-8254-3269-3 **208 pp.** paperback

Twelve Great Questions About Christ Clarence E. Macartney
Macartney addresses commonly asked questions about the life and person of Jesus Christ. The integrity of the Scriptures underlies the provocative answers that Dr. Macartney provides in this thoughtful book. The broad range of subject matter will inform and inspire laymen and clergy alike as they peruse these pages.

ISBN 0-8254-3267-7 **160 pp.** paperback

Treasury of the World's Great Sermons Warren W. Wiersbe
These outstanding sermons are presented from 122 of the greatest preachers. A short biographical sketch of every preacher is also included. Complete with an index of texts and sermons.
ISBN 0-8254-4002-5   672 double-column pp.   paperback

Classic Sermons on the Attributes of God Warren W. Wiersbe
These classic sermons lay a solid foundation for the study of God's attributes such as truth, holiness, sovereignty, omnipresence, immutability, and love. Includes messages by Henry Ward Beecher, J. D. Jones, J. H. Jowett, D. L. Moody, and John Wesley.
ISBN 0-8254-4038-6   160 pp.   paperback

Classic Sermons on the Birth of Christ Warren W. Wiersbe
The central theme of the Bible is expanded and expounded in this collection of sermons from such great preachers as Henry P. Liddon, Walter A. Maier, G. Campbell Morgan, Arthur T. Pierson, and James S. Stewart.
ISBN 0-8254-4044-0   160 pp.   paperback

Classic Sermons on Christian Service Warren W. Wiersbe
Dynamic principles for Christian service will be found in these classic sermons by highly acclaimed pulpit masters. Warren W. Wiersbe has carefully selected sermons which describe the essential characteristics of Christian servanthood.
ISBN 0-8254-4041-6   160 pp.   paperback

Classic Sermons on the Cross of Christ Warren W. Wiersbe
An inspiring collection of sermons on perhaps the most significant event the world ever experienced—the cross of Christ. Through masterful sermons by great pulpit masters, the reader will gain a greater understanding of the theological, devotional, and practical importance of the cross of Christ.
ISBN 0-8254-4040-8   160 pp.   paperback

Classic Sermons on Faith and Doubt Warren W. Wiersbe
A collection of 12 carefully selected sermons, the goal of which is to stimulate the growth and maturity of the believer's faith. Among the preachers represented are A. C. Dixon, J. H. Jowett, D. Martyn Lloyd-Jones, G. Campbell Morgan, and Martin Luther.
ISBN 0-8254-4028-9   160 pp.   paperback

Classic Sermons on Family and Home Warren W. Wiersbe
The erosion of traditional family and biblical values is accelerating at an alarming rate. Dr. Wiersbe has compiled *Classic Sermons on Family and Home* to help recapture God's enduring truth for the family today.
ISBN 0-8254-4054-8   160 pp.   paperback

Classic Sermons on Hope Warren W. Wiersbe
Crime. Poverty. Disease. War. Social upheaval. Ecological disaster. Warren W. Wiersbe has chosen twelve classic sermons on hope that will encourage the reader to face struggles with a confident Christian hope. Included are sermons by G. Campbell Morgan, D. L. Moody, Charles Spurgeon, and A. W. Tozer. Excellent starter material for sermon preparation; solid spiritual content for devotional readers.
ISBN 0-8254-4045-9   160 pp.   paperback

Classic Sermons on the Names of God Warren W. Wiersbe
Any study of the names of God in Scripture will be enhanced by the classic sermons included in this collection. They feature sermons from Charles H. Spurgeon, G. Campbell Morgan, John Ker, George Morrison, Alexander MacLaren, and George Whitefield.
ISBN 0-8254-4052-1   **160 pp.**   **paperback**

Classic Sermons on Overcoming Fear Warren W. Wiersbe
Classic sermons by such famous preachers as Alexander Maclaren, V. Raymond Edman, Clarence Macartney, George H. Morrison, Charles H. Spurgeon, George W. Truett and others. Wiersbe has chosen sermons which offer insight as well as hope for believers faced with the uncertainty of this pilgrim journey.
ISBN 0-8254-4043-2   **160 pp.**   **paperback**

Classic Sermons on Prayer Warren W. Wiersbe
Fourteen pulpit giants present the need for and the results of a life permeated with prayer. These sermons by such famous preachers as Dwight L. Moody, G. Campbell Morgan, Charles H. Spurgeon, Reuben A. Torrey, Alexander Whyte, and others, will help you experience the strength and power of God in prayer.
ISBN 0-8254-4029-7   **160 pp.**   **paperback**

Classic Sermons on the Prodigal Son Warren W. Wiersbe
These sermons by highly acclaimed pulpit masters offer unique insights into perhaps the most famous of Christ's parables. These sermons will provide new understanding of the relationships between the son, father and other son. Believers will also be challenged to apply the wonderful truth of the Father's love to their own lives.
ISBN 0-8254-4039-4   **160 pp.**   **paperback**

Classic Sermons on the Resurrection of Christ Warren W. Wiersbe
These sermons represent the best in scholarship, warmed by deep inspiration and enlivened by excitement about what the Resurrection of Christ means to the believer.
ISBN 0-8254-4042-4   **160 pp.**   **paperback**

Classic Sermons on the Second Coming and
Other Prophetic Themes Warren W. Wiersbe
The second coming of Christ is a promise presented in many New Testament passages. Dr. Wiersbe has marshaled an array of classic sermons on Christ's coming by great preachers such as C. H. Spurgeon, G. Campbell Morgan, C. E. Macartney, and Alexander MacLaren.
ISBN 0-8254-4051-3   **160 pp.**   **paperback**

Classic Sermons on the Sovereignty of God Warren W. Wiersbe
Sovereignty. All authority, power, dominion, and majesty belong to God. Warren W. Wiersbe has chosen twelve classic sermons that capture the glory and grace of this divine attribute. Included are sermons by Paul Little, R. A. Torrey, C. H. Spurgeon, and Jonathon Edwards. Excellent starter material for sermon preparation; solid spiritual content for devotional readers.
0-8254-4055-6   **160 pp.**   **paperback**

Classic Sermons on Spiritual Warfare Warren W. Wiersbe
In a timely new compilation of classic sermons, Dr. Warren Wiersbe offers eleven expositions dealing with various facets of Satanic activity. Included are sermons by such outstanding preachers as William Culbertson, Allan Redpath, D. Martyn Lloyd-Jones, G. Campbell Morgan, and C. H. Spurgeon.
ISBN 0-8254-4049-1   **160 pp.**   **paperback**